Conversatic

BENTLEY

The Cosmic, Conservationist Cat

Insights from a Cat in Heaven about

Life, Death & Saving the Planet

Clare Metcalf

& Janet Barber (Bentley's Mum)

First paperback edition printed 2024 in the United Kingdom
ISBN - 978-1-910815304

A catalogue recorded for this book is available from the British Library.

Published by Mystic Mouse Publishing
www.mysticmouse.com
Designed by Lorenzo Guescini / Mystic Mouse Design
www.lorenzoguescini.com
Photo/Art Credits
Page 46: Tiger © Lorenzo Guescini, 2016
Page 49: White Lions © Lorenzo Guescini, 2014
Page 91: Blue Footed Boobies photo © Haha used courtesy of Pexels.com
Page 109: Elephant Calf & Mother © Grobler du Preez/under license Shutterstock.com
Page 130: Lennox © Clare Metcalf
Page 148: Peace Fire art © Clare Metcalf, 2024
Page 162: Nacreous Cloud photo © Clare Metcalf, 2024
All Bentley & Pippin pictures supplied by Janet Barber and used with permission
Certain decorative elements used under license from DesignCuts.com

‘I dedicate this book to Family; my beloved Mother, who I chose as my mother because we needed each other. I led her to Clare, who has become family, as I have seen fit to share all my wisdom with her. And we have our own family in Heaven that you, dear reader, are about to meet – which in turn makes YOU family.

You didn’t come to this book by accident. You are one of us. And I dedicate my words to you to encourage and support you with my stories of enduring love, commitment and hope. Read it in its entirety, or dip into it as an oracle of hope whenever you need light in your day.’

Bentley

1 APRIL 1993 – 11 MAY 2011

To Danielle
Trust your spirit guides, especially those with paws, feathers, fins or scales – they will never let you down.
Your heart is decorated with paw prints.
Love
Clare
x

Bentley chose ch12 as your special message.
x

Index

Foreword

Just Ask Bentley!

Have you ever wanted to sit down with an Ascended Master and ask every question you can think of about life, death, altered states of human consciousness and their practical applications in our day to day lives? Or about the salvation of the ecology of our beautiful Mother Earth, and the role of animals in human evolution? And what about other star systems?

Of course, there are many sources of channeled information, from master teachers to angelic beings from whom you may glean insights about the mysteries of the Universe. So, who would you ask? Archangel Raphael? Christ? Mother Mary? Quan Yin? Ganesha? Buddha even?

Well, there's a new avatar in town. Just ask Bentley!

This is a collection of channeled readings with an Ascended Master, lovingly compiled by expert animal communicator, and admittedly, one of my favorite students of all time, Clare Metcalf. In this book mysteries are revealed in movie script style as Janet, the human soulmate of master Bentley, asks fascinating questions of this disembodied avatar. Bentley is now an angelic guide not only for his favorite human, but for the entire human race!

What makes these readings and conversations so magical? Bentley not only has a halo, he has whiskers! Who better than a cat to reveal that cosmic consciousness comes in furry forms too!

How easily our spirit guides can be overlooked when they appear to us as little purring packages of blissed-out unconditional love. But don't let the Earthly forms fool you! Bentley's soul has access to information and guidance for his grieving mom, Janet, that suggests that life-after-death is not only a reality, but simply a doorway between dimensions. The only way for us to see through the shadows of blinding grief is to raise our frequency, open our hearts and minds, and put our disbelief aside.

Let Bentley teach you about the exquisite nature of the dance of souls throughout the Universe, and rest assured your loved ones will somewhere, one day soon dance right back into your loving arms.

I've had many students walk through the doors to my Animal Communication classes over the last 34 years, but there was one in particular who actually helped facilitate my workshops in the UK for seven consecutive years. There was something special about this one. This one had a heart like an oasis in the desert. Even I, as her teacher, was drawn to her, to let my spirit drink in her ready-made bevy of beverages for the spirit; hope, warmth, compassion, wisdom, a spirit of adventure to learn more and more, and a ringing laugh that would put any amount of elves to shame.

Over those seven years and on into the present moment, I watched Clare Metcalf trouble-shoot an endless array of animal/human problems. From bittersweet to downright hilarious, I've seen her solve dating issues amongst bears (yes, that's right folks! Bears!) to unrequited love between lonely pigs, to countless 'readings' where she's operated not only as an ambassador between species, but even as a priestess who can relay messages between animals in Heaven to humans back down here on Earth. Psychic ability is an incredibly comforting thing, it really is, especially when the psychic can translate for you the messages from an animal whose loss hurt you so deeply you thought the wound would never mend.

As one of my most celebrated certified students, I trust Clare wholeheartedly because her talent is now backed-up with decades of accurate readings where physical conditions were accurately identified and behavior and relationship problems were solved between both humans and animals, and between animals and animals, plus messages were relayed all the way from Heaven that helped ease minds and heal broken hearts. Clare Metcalf is the real deal, tried and true, as an ambassador between species, as hundreds (if not thousands) of her own clients and students will attest. I've seen and read of her successes with my own eyes for almost 20 years now, but in this book, she's relaying wisdom from a cat in Heaven who may be 'dead' but still has a *lot* on his mind!

I know every word of this book is true, because Clare used to be the go-between on occasion even with my own feline angels. Nothing was more convincing than when I'd be in the US and receive an email from Clare:

'Flo's here'. Uh-oh. Cover your ears!

And then, there would be the telling-off that always followed, not just of my weaknesses, but of Clare's too. My cantankerous little black and white broad of a cat, Florabelle (or Ol' Aunt Flo as I affectionately called her,) died 15 years ago, and I'd never told Clare that Flo's 'voice in my head' always blasted in like an old movie star's, barking orders in a gravelly shout, demanding that we thick humans listen to our spirit guides no matter what shape they embodied on Earth. Flo took it upon herself to not only advise me from her higher vantage point, but she'd blow her torch onto Clare too, especially if she felt she needed to warn Clare about something or guide her in a safer direction.

Cats. Honestly. Dead or alive, what would we do without their tutelage?

If this book is in your hands, it could be that your heart is utterly shattered by the loss of an animal you loved. Are you wondering if they're truly gone forever? Are you hoping with all your heart you can find a way to 'hear' them, maybe even 'see' them but most certainly 'feel' them one more time?

If so, someone has now come into your existence who can open your mind to new paradigms, open your heart to new levels of comfort, peace, hope & joy, and she'll tickle your funny bone too.

She doesn't have four legs like the one who broke your heart. She has two. But her ability to teach you how to listen to animals in Heaven is laced throughout the story of one of her client's cats, who is a master teacher in his own right – I've never met a cat who wasn't! This two-legged wonder of a woman can open your eyes to another world, a world so full of beauty, magic and endless love, she might be able to lift your spirits, broaden your horizons, and maybe even fan your burning pain with her huge white wings.

Welcome to Clare Metcalf's world. You'll find that there's a reason Clare can channel angels. It's because… well… she is one.

Amelia Kinkade, author of 6 books including the bestseller, Straight From the Horse's Mouth: How to Talk to Animals and Get Answers (Random House, Harper Collins, New World Library), The Language of Miracles: A Celebrated Psychic Teaches You to Talk to Animals (New World Library), and Whispers from the Wild: Listening to Messages From the Animal Kingdom (New World Library). Amelia is also the founder of Amelia's Ark Angel Society, a charity that educates children in rural Africa about poaching vs. protecting wild animals.

Preface

Heart to Heart Connections

It seems relatively easy to strike up friendships with people when there is an animal involved. People with dogs get to know other people with dogs while walking by the river or on the common, or wherever they may choose to wander. People with cats have various different ways. There is, of course, the banging on a complete stranger's door to ask permission to plough through their garden shrubbery because your cat has not returned home when they should have done, even though you know jolly well that if your cat does not wish to be found they will make sure that they aren't.

Then someone else with a cat will bang on your door for the same reason because they know their cat uses your garden whenever they can get away with it.

Another point of contact is the pet food section at the supermarket. Cat people have a habit of standing for considerable lengths of time in silence staring at what is on offer, with a look of dismay on their faces. Eventually someone breaks the silence and utters that well known phrase 'My cat is so fussy about their food.' That of course means fussy about what is on offer to them, not fussy about what they may drag in through the cat flap from outside.

Enough to say that anyone who lives with a cat learns that when getting up in the morning the first thing to do is put on slippers because you're never sure what you will come across. It is also useful to add disposable gloves to the shopping list!

Cats have long been regarded as mysterious creatures, often appearing to possess an otherworldly wisdom. Many cat lovers have experienced those moments of uncanny connection with their feline companions – whether it's a knowing look, a comforting purr at just the right moment, or the feeling that their cat understands far more than they let on. But what if these connections could continue even after a cat's physical presence has departed? What if the love and communication you shared with your pet could extend into the afterlife?

Conversations with Bentley – The Cosmic Conservationist Cat is a journey into the mystical and profound world of animal communication, where a cat's voice reaches across the veil to impart knowledge and predictions that are as enchanting as they are enlightening. Through a narrative that intertwines three different voices, this book invites you to explore the wonders of the unseen, the messages that come from beyond, and the deep connections we share with our animal friends.

In a world where the boundaries between life and death are often seen as rigid and unyielding, there exists a realm where the spirits of our beloved companions continue to thrive, offering wisdom, comfort, and guidance. This is a story of one such spirit – Bentley, a little black cat who, from the other side, continues to share his insights and experiences, reminding us that the bond between humans and animals transcends the physical world.

Bentley's story is one of heart to heart connections, conservation, and the enduring spirit of a cat who continues to care for the world, even from Heaven. Through this book, you will be taken on a journey where the extraordinary becomes ordinary, where communication with animals is not limited to this life, and where the wisdom of a little black cat can open your eyes to the magic that surrounds us. Through Bentley's cosmic perspective, you will find that the world is full of surprises, lessons, and, above all… love.

Conversations with a Cosmic Conservationist Cat

Chapter 1

Meant to Be

Clare, the Animal Communicator

Clare: I sat gazing at the photo of the bright-eyed black cat in his prime. He had no obvious unique features or markings aside from his glowing amber eyes and there were no clues from his body as to what might have ailed him in his final days on Earth.

As soon as I saw his earnest expression, I could see he was eager to talk. He had that 'buzzing' kind of energy we sometimes feel when we're about to embark on a *really* exciting adventure, and his expression told me this cat had a lot to say for himself and that he had chosen *me* to be his interpreter.

My gaze softened, I drew a deep, steadying breath and a huge wave of love emanated from my heart to his. That's the connection; the signal or wavelength we use to connect with all other creatures telepathically. They recognise the frequency, acknowledging that it comes from another being wishing to make contact with them, and they respond to it – much like answering a ringing telephone.

When you contact an animal from a place of love, they reciprocate.

It was January 2012 and I had received a request from Janet to communicate with her beloved cat Bentley who had passed to Spirit in May 2011. It's a genuine honour to be asked to help reconnect someone with their loved ones in Spirit, and something I don't take lightly. I know I've been entrusted to gently hold their broken heart and try to begin their healing process by being as sensitive, empathic, and accurate as possible in my communications. I also need to be open to hearing anything the animal wishes their people to know.

Like most people who approach me for this kind of work, Janet wanted to know if Bentley had crossed over safely, how he was 'feeling' since then and if he needed to tell her anything…

Janet, Bentley's Mum

> **Janet:** I could say that Bentley and I got together by accident. I could, but I don't think that would be true. I wanted to move home and had found just the right place about twelve miles away. There was only one problem, it was not for sale. Four years later the property came on the market and I snapped it up. I first met Bentley shortly after settling in and later discovered he had moved next door as a kitten, just about the time I had first set eyes on the home I wanted!
>
> I would see Bentley around a lot, sometimes in my garden, sometimes on the pathway at the front. We did not get on because he did not like women. Over the next few years he learned to tolerate me and sometimes we would even have a quick chat. Well, I would chat and he would ignore me; zoning out might be a better way of expressing it.
>
> He was always a much-loved cat, but sometimes circumstances change and that is what happened when Bentley was nine and a half years old. His Dad moved house and Bentley went too. However,

for reasons best known to himself, Bentley was not about to give up his old territory easily. In part I feel this was because his new home area already had an abundance of cats and they were not about to surrender anything to the new cat on the block, so this caused much heartache. His Dad loved him too much to force him to stay somewhere he did not want to be and by that time I loved Bentley enough to let him stay with me, but he and his Dad remained close forever.

Bentley moved in, gently and carefully. We circled around each other for a while, both mentally and physically. I was not his owner. No one ever owned Bentley. I was not his carer – he did not need one. He was, and is, a Free Spirit but chose to make my home his own, because he wanted to, and that was the start of the most amazing eight and a half years.

At some point I went from merely being a boarding house landlady, to foster Mum and eventually, happily, to Mum. We were best friends, and everything was right in my world as long as he was a part of it. I was told when to go outside and do some work in the garden. We did it together, Bentley supervising. When he decided I had done enough for the day he made it quite clear I could down tools and relax. He liked everything in the house to be in order; such things as decorating were a little frowned upon, but accepted providing all was set back in place at the end of each day. We were a 50/50 team, or maybe a 60/40 team in his favour. We did not care, we worked together.

Bentley was never out to impress anyone; he didn't have to. He was special. I wanted it to last forever but eventually, as always happens, Bentley was called to Rainbow Bridge; that place where our beloved animals must go when their time has come.

My world was empty. My best and dearest friend had gone. He who understood my every thought and action and made everything right.

A couple of weeks later, I (not a particularly spiritual person) realised this was far from the end. Bentley was keeping in touch in various and unbelievable ways. Was something wrong? Somehow, I had to reach him. I tried mediums with no success and then in desperation I looked on the internet for animal communicators, found Clare Metcalf and liked what I saw. Her photograph showed someone kind and understanding, and I felt she was the right person. I made contact and asked if she could talk to animals that have died. She confirmed that it was exactly the same as talking with an animal who was alive. So, Clare entered my world.

I explained how worried I was about Bentley because I felt that something was wrong adding, **'You may not be able to find him and if you do, he may just tell you to go away. I doubt he will say a lot, he was never much of a talker.'**

The 'Psychic Call'

So here I was, holding the photo of a very handsome, yet seemingly unassuming and unremarkable cat, and asking him the questions his Mum so desperately needed answers to. Once we were deep in conversation however, I soon realised this little black cat with the glowing amber eyes, a sprinkling of white hairs on his chest and cute little paws was, indeed, remarkable!

Before any communication session, I ask to be supplied with basic information; name, gender, age, and species. (Oh yes, I've been sent photos and wondered, 'What kind of creature *is* this?') I also ask for one or two photos of the animal's face where I can see their features clearly, as that's the instrument I use to make the connection. It's my 'psychic telephone' if you like!

Any questions need to be open, and worded in such a manner I can't begin to guess the animal's story. There are two reasons for this; the brain can start to formulate responses even before connecting with the animal, plus I need the humans by the end of the session to know they did not give me any clues or suggest any of the things their animal shared with me. That's the only way to guarantee their peace of mind and for them to experience the sheer joy of knowing they really did hear from their beloved animal in Spirit.

Safe in the knowledge that Bentley had picked up my 'psychic call', I began.

'Hi Bentley. My name is Clare, and your Mum Janet has asked me to speak with you to find out how you are and to see if you have any messages for her.'

Instantly, as soon as I'd uttered my introduction, an excited, well-spoken voice of indiscriminate age inside my head replied,

> 'I told her I'd be back. I wouldn't abandon her forever. But tell her, don't ask anyone else about me – what do they know? Ask ME. The Stately Panther. Stealthy and solitary. King of all I surveyed. Independent, to the last. Look at me, a Jaguar, sleek and handsome and restored to my former glory. Coat gleaming once again, all my teeth intact. Claws like razor blades.'

Bentley, restored to perfection, didn't want 'human psychic mediums' trying to contact him and ask questions, he had been waiting for this opportunity, to speak for himself, directly to his Mum.

In order to convince the client I am communicating with their own animal, I may ask for some physical signs or symptoms of what was happening in their body prior to passing over. No upsetting details, but it's important to be able to differentiate between accident or injury and chronic illness or old age. Bentley provided enough detail to convince Janet this was indeed her beloved cat, without unduly upsetting her. Bentley then informed me that he had visited Janet on several occasions – at least eight times since he had passed.

> 'She has seen me out of the corner of her eye. Brushing past her legs. Sitting in my usual place on the windowsill. I spoke in her dreams. How can she think I'd go and never come back? No cords can be cut from heart to heart, from chest to chest.'

Bentley beamed to me a heart-warming image of himself sitting on Janet's chest, exchanging that frequency of love in a quiet, blissful moment.

> 'We remain connected. I'm not with the Old Folk (Mum's family in Spirit). Why would I be? We all have our own destinies and ours aren't linked. I don't need anyone to take care of me.'

In our feedback call, Janet confided that she had been terribly worried that Bentley might have been with her parents, which was certainly not her wish for his eternity. Bentley continued, a slight indignant tone in his voice,

> 'It was SHE who encouraged me to be independent, my own 'man' if you like. Why would she expect my Spirit to become dependent on anyone? Indeed, why should her parent's Spirits be dependent on me? I don't mean a great deal to them and vice versa. They didn't even know me in life.
>
> I thought about coming back (reincarnating in physical form) but now I have a job. I'm with a young girl in Spirit who needs a friend and someone to show her unconditional love. She's very pretty but she's solemn, a loner. We relate.'

Bentley showed me the image of a pretty young girl with shiny, light brown hair, the colour of a field mouse, cut into a shoulder length bob with a fringe. She had downcast dark grey-blue eyes and was wearing a terribly sad expression which rapidly changed to joy on the arrival of her new feline friend.

Bentley explained that the girl had died young and that none of her relatives or loved ones were yet in Spirit, so he had been assigned to keep her company until she had a human Spirit to take over.

> 'But my dear Mother, that does not mean you no longer matter to me.
>
> I also want you to know that it wasn't that I had a short attention span, I just found other things more fascinating than listening to you witter on about nothing all day! And your 'singing'! Oh, my word, it scared the crows!'

After allowing me a moment to have a titter about his critical review of his Mum's singing, Bentley explained,

> 'In my prime I looked like Bagheera from The Jungle Book. But I didn't appreciate nicknames or sentimentality. She's quite intuitive and is on the 'alternative' path but some of her ideas are a bit cock-eyed! Tell her to focus on the moon for guidance and the stream for tranquillity. Don't believe everything everyone tells you. Never trust an ego, even though at times I appeared to be Ego Personified! I could also be quite benevolent and friendly. But the smoke! My goodness I did NOT like the smoke! There MUST be something better than that, surely? Flippin' catnip is better than THAT stuff!'

Janet sheepishly admitted to me that she knew Bentley had been disapproving of her smoking habit, and as you'll discover, he wasn't particularly enticed by catnip either!

Here I should explain about the use of capitals etc. in Bentley's conversations. When I communicate with animals, I focus on the photo of them and sit with a notepad and pen, basically ready to take dictation from the animal. It becomes like a form of Automatic Writing as they guide my pen and I try my best to stop my brain becoming engaged (the brain forms thoughts and questions about subjects that are, for the most part, none of my business; this message is between the animal and their beloved human, I'm simply the person who holds the pen!)

As Bentley speaks with me and I'm busily recording his words, he decides on any inflections and exclamations within his sentences, and as far as possible I've punctuated the sentences exactly as he speaks to me, so you may 'hear his voice' so to speak. So, if a word begins with a capital letter, that usually denotes a role, a job or purpose, for example when an animal tells me their role is 'Guardian Angel' or 'Peace-Keeper'. Words in italics are to be emphasised and words in capitals are VERY important either for emphasis or description, and I must not omit or change them! So, as his story unfolds you will see there are some statements which are incredibly important to Bentley, and therefore to us, his readers and followers.

Bentley continued,

> 'I did love the Great Outdoors and the smell of flowers and plants, and even the taste of some.'

At this point I became completely enveloped in the sweet, slightly woody and soothing aroma of lavender flowers. Janet explained that Bentley really enjoyed sleeping by the lavender shrub in the garden.

He then showed me an image of a patch of large, white daisies, completely flattened by him sleeping and rolling in them. As I was soon to discover, these were the infamous Dog Daisies belonging to a neighbour!

> 'I approve of the new cat visitor, though my personality was stronger! Yes, I'm arrogant and opinionated. I'll say it again, LOOK AT ME!'

I smiled, 'Yes Bentley, you're magnificent!'

> 'Tell Mum we were together in a previous life in the Savannah. I was spotted. A Serval Cat. She was a Native tribesman, and we became friends. I chose to be his companion. He was killed while still young by other tribespeople – betrayed by them. Killed by an arrow or a spear. It's why she has trouble trusting and why she finds it hard to forgive. Her feeling of "don't stab me in the back". Our lives will be entwined again, whether in this life or the next I don't yet know. I am needed by the young girl for now until she has some human Spirits to accompany her. However, needless to say, our paths will cross again, and we will know each other.
>
> Now I'm off. She knows I love her. I don't need to tell her. I'm here in the garden whenever she needs me.'

As Bentley drew his energy back and away from me, indicating the close of our conversation, (hanging up the Psychic Telephone!) he showed me an image of the deep Mediterranean blue, gold flecked crystal, Lapis Lazuli. Usually, if the animal is in Spirit, items mentioned in this way can be relevant to the human receiving the messages. Unable to leave them as physical gifts for their loved ones, sometimes it's an invitation for their people to learn more about the items or to acquire them for themselves if they feel particularly drawn to them and the reasons behind the 'gift'.

And if you don't believe me, just ask one of my clients whose horse developed a 'very expensive crystal habit' (her words) amassing dozens of colourful, sparkling, and powerful crystals in their stable!

Lapis Lazuli is a crystal that is believed to release stress, replacing it with peace, harmony, and deep inner knowledge, providing qualities of honesty, compassion and morality. It may help us speak our truth, filling us with confidence, and cementing relationships, aiding in expressing our feelings and emotions.

At the time, neither Janet nor I had any clue that subsequent communications would cement Janet and Bentley's relationship (or indeed Janet's and mine, and Bentley's and mine), or that he would inspire us both to take on the mantle of compassion and morality for all living creatures in his name, and ultimately encourage Janet to speak hers and Bentley's truth with confidence and in ways she never dreamed possible. Neither of us ever thought we'd be writing a book together that's for sure!

So, as I phoned Janet to tell her the messages her beautiful boy had for her, for me this was just another day in the office. Little was I to know that we were about to embark on an incredible journey of exploration and education with this soft, sleek, velvety pawed, miniature black panther with an independent nature and a forceful will to be heard!

Janet: I was left in no doubt after the first conversation with Clare that I was indeed receiving messages from Bentley. He explained what had happened to him to cause him to cross over and so many other familiar things. He also admitted to crushing those darned Dog Daisies!

I clearly remember the time my neighbour called me over to take a look at the huge patch of Dog Daisies in her back garden that had been flattened! Bentley came too, to inspect the object of the complaint.

'A cat has done that', she said.

I looked at Bentley and he stared back at me… I knew!

'Mmmm, a very large patch for a little cat', I pointed out, 'I think that may have been a fox'.

My neighbour accepted the suggestion and we left.

'Come along Bentley.' One rigid black tail pointing skyward on the retreating end of an unabashed-faced black cat can speak a thousand words!

Bentley even shared with Clare the 'pet' name I had for him, which was Bub.

So that was the start of a relationship with Bentley on a whole different level. He who had taught me so much when he was with me, was about to teach me so much more.

Bentley continues to educate and encourage me. He also ticks me off when he thinks it necessary. I keep all the records of his words so I can make sure his teachings are heard by a wider audience. Why else did he bring Clare and I together? Because we are his scribes!

As Bentley says, 'paws can only play with pens, not hold them.'

He wants this to be a collaborative effort. Although he is, and always will be, special to Clare and to me, he has decided his words and teachings are to reach a wider audience.

He wants you to know that it's not just a black hole after leaving the physical body.

He wants you to discover the magical journey that awaits us all.

I have always been so very proud of Bentley and honoured that he chose to spend part of his life on Earth with me. He has my love and my respect. He was not my pet, and I did not own him. No one has the right to own anyone. He was and is my friend and family. I value every minute we spent together and all the memories, of which only a few have been mentioned here in this book. I was however not quite happy about 'going public' with my chats with Bentley. I had always considered them a very private part of my life. I spoke to him about my concerns. Bentley's answer was simple and straightforward:

> 'One day they will all be thrown away and then no one will ever know!'

Interspecies Telepathic Communication

All living beings are born with the ability to communicate telepathically. It's how mothers instinctively know when their babies are ill, uncomfortable, or unhappy. It's how infants communicate with each other, and how animals establish pack hierarchy, social circles, behaviour, and boundaries. For humans it can be thinking of someone and seconds later they call you, or simply having a 'feeling' about someone that turns out to be true.

Since I use a form of telepathy involving connection with the energy of the subject, it is perfectly possible to communicate with animals who have left their physical bodies, because their energy carries on outside the physical vehicle of the body. The process of communicating is the same and just as effective if the animal is living or already in Spirit.

This is known as Interspecies Telepathic Communication, or quite simply… Animal Communication.

My main skill is clairaudience, i.e. I can hear the actual words spoken by all animals. It's not like watching a film with their mouths moving, (how disappointing for my home visit clients, who seem to be expecting to witness some great miracle!) I just hear their telepathic messages.

I tune in to their unique heart resonance, their Soul's unique vibration, which is simpler than it sounds, and once they learn my methods my students are always astonished when they know they've connected with an animal for the first time. With practice it becomes easier to tune out our own mental chatter, slow the brainwaves and match our heart resonance closely with the pattern emitted by the animal. It's much like tuning in a radio for the clearest and sharpest broadcast. Once one becomes proficient at this, the messages generally come through extremely quickly and clearly, and sometimes with shocking, funny or unexpected information!

We all have our own 'internal voice' – the one that criticises, guides, and corrects us frequently throughout the day, but the voice of animals isn't that. It sounds and feels different, often well-spoken, articulate, and it rarely has a Geordie accent (like mine), so I know it's coming from an animal and that it's not based within my own imagination!

When I communicate with an animal, I report back word for word what I have heard, without attempting to interpret anything or put my own spin on it, as it's not my information to interpret. I am simply the 'Psychic PA' taking the minutes of our conversation to pass them on in their entirety to their human. The messages are between the animal and their human; they're not meant to necessarily mean anything to me. As long as it makes sense to the animal's human, all is good.

Note: I don't use the term 'owner' as I find it demeaning, since no-one can own another being, another Soul. So, humans will be referred to as humans, parents, or as family, however the animal feels about them.

If the animal doesn't know the word or name for something they may try to describe it verbally, show me an image of it (Clairvoyance), allow me to access the physical sensations such as pain or discomfort (Clairsentience) let me feel the emotion around the concept (Clairempathy) or sometimes taste or smell it! (Clairgustance and Clairalience). Let's just say that because of this, some communications are more enjoyable than others, and they're always informative, often entertaining and sometimes downright astonishing!

Chapter 2

Broken Hearts Expand

I had a feeling that the original chat I had with Bentley and Janet would not be the last, but it's not my job to put that idea into people's heads. Some people become entranced by the whole concept of being able to continue their relationship with their beloved animals even when they can no longer see them. And some animals just seem to have a lot to say. So, when I received an email from Janet asking to set up another appointment to hear from Bentley, I was rather looking forward to hearing what the little black feline had to say for himself. His personality had been so strong in his first communication, his presence so determined and precise, and Janet's reaction had been so joyful in hearing from her beloved boy again that I knew it was going to be interesting and I secretly wondered if Janet was bracing herself for what he might tell her, in his forthright manner!

I settled down with his photo and re-introduced myself, explaining that Janet, his Mum, was wondering how he was doing now and if he needed to tell her anything new.

> 'First of all, I want you to tell my Mum that I decide where I go and who I'm with. I pop in on my Mum and my territory from time to time. What does she think my visits are all about? A punishment for me? Some sense of duty or even politeness? No, my visits are all about heart connections, freedom and happiness. She's nuts if she thinks I would spend time with someone I don't want to and I know she wouldn't do that either.'

It turned out that Janet had been feeling guilty, thinking that by wanting to continue communicating with Bentley, she might be keeping him attached to her in some way. She was concerned she might be preventing him from 'moving on' or doing something more important with his time than spending it in her company. Bentley was clear to reassure her, in his no-nonsense style, that he would not attach himself to her out of any sense of duty or politeness, because in reality these were not exactly qualities he admired – and he had recognised the same feeling in Janet.

He also wanted to reassure her that he was not expected to be attached to any of the people she had known who were already in Spirit.

I have learned from the animals that family ties, friends or acquaintances only connect with each other in Heaven if there is also a heart connection – a love that transcends life and death, that keeps us together for all eternity. If that loving bond was not shared in this life, it does not become obligatory in the next. Neither do their souls feel obliged to hang around us while we're still living. We have no obligation to stay with family or acquaintances we had no real connection with when we reach the afterlife. However, if there is that heart connection, the next life is blissful!

How beautiful that this independent and rather forceful cat should tell us that he chooses to visit his Mum because they have a heart connection and that he has the freedom to choose what to do with his time and who to spend it with, yet he finds happiness in visiting and spending time at home with her.

Janet asked me to reassure Bentley that he had not been replaced in her affections by one of the neighbour's cats who had taken to visiting her, now that Bentley was no longer physically able to defend his territory. She needn't have worried…

> 'I do know she doesn't have another cat, does she think I'm stupid? I know who Dave is. Why would I object to her having company and

opening her heart to someone else? I'm a bit offended that she thinks I'm THAT egotistical, after all I have company and friendship, so why shouldn't she? It would be too cruel to insist that she didn't. The heart expands for ALL new love that enters it. I am going to send her a stray cat and they will end up Soul Mates. The new cat will be in a mess, with some white on him, but she won't notice that at first.'

Janet: Pippin, who came along later did indeed have some white on him – a little at the throat as so many black cats have, and just one white hair on his chin!

Bentley was explaining in his own inimitable style that it's natural and healthy to seek the affection of others when we have lost a loved one and that it's actually unhealthy to close off the heart and wallow in mournfulness. His explanation that the heart simply expands to accommodate all the new love it needs to receive and to give, even when it's been broken, has been a comfort to many of my clients since.

I do sometimes share, anonymously and with permission of course, snippets of wisdom and advice from the animals I work with, which so many of my clients find incredibly comforting. That support from another animal in their grief is such a wonderful gift to receive.

'Tell her she is a berk. She is so worried about everyone that has gone before instead of living in the now. Let the Souls in Spirit do their own thing. Make this the best life you can have. Experience everything. Life is all about balance. There's no reason to be lonely just because you're missing someone. Those gone before want you to be happy. You have a loving heart, patience and understanding. It does not mean that I love you any less or that you love me any less.'

I asked Bentley if there were any ways he could let Janet know he was around her; signs she may recognise that might console and comfort her.

> 'Last Sunday, I manifested myself as a rather persistent bee in the garden. I've also appeared to her as the black bird shouting at her for attention.'

Janet began to laugh as I described this to her, exclaiming,

'Boy did that bird shout, it was a crow, but I thought I was singing to myself at the time!'

The mental image of Janet (who Bentley had already declared to be not the best singer in the world) and the sleek black cawing, head-bobbing crow, harmonising like some strange, other worldly Sonny and Cher is one that tickles me to this day!

> 'I have decided to send the stray cat to her when she is ready but I will decide when and where.'

Janet was a little horrified at this news, because she was still very much grieving for Bentley, and she didn't feel ready to let anyone new into her life; and was unsure she ever would. I reassured her that Bentley would know if and when the time was right for her, and for the cat that would eventually arrive looking for a home and space in her expanding heart. I hear this time and again from my grieving clients, and even when there's some resistance to the newcomer at first, it always turns out to be true Divine Timing when they find each other.

'What else would you like your Mum to know, Bentley?'

> 'I do hear everything she says to me. Silly, silly old Mum.'

Bentley's voice became so soft and affectionate at this point, his expression so wistful, that my eyes filled with tears, feeling the emotion behind his words about his beloved Mum. Even though this dynamo of a cat had many lessons and chastisements for his Mum over the years to come, they were all anchored in his deep love and devotion to her.

> 'I do still sit on your chest. Your chest is good for sitting on. I know you miss stroking my cheeks and I miss it too.'

Bentley turned his gaze to me and stated,

> 'Dave did something I used to do and it surprised her. That was me sending her a message.'

Dave was the neighbour's cat previously mentioned, and I asked Janet if she could recall him doing this.

> **Janet:** I remember it well, something Dave never does but Bentley always did. I would be stroking him, and he would put his head down into my hand and then jerk his head back so that my hand would go to the top of his head, as if to say scratch me there please.

When Bentley says 'that was me' what he means is he was influencing Dave to take on one of his own peculiar habits so Janet would recognise it, and know it was a sign from him.

Occasionally animals allow one in Spirit to do what I call a 'pop in'. Once we leave our physical bodies we return to pure energy (the Soul or Spirit in many belief systems) and energy can be anywhere and everywhere, therefore it's a simple process to enter into another organism for a brief moment in time, to send a message or grab your human's attention. Many people have reported to me that they have seen a stray animal, only briefly, after their beloved pet has died. The animal completely grabs their attention, making eye contact, connecting, but later vanishes never to return. I firmly believe these are visitations from our newly passed over pets.

One client had engaged my services to help find her missing rooster. I had the sad task of informing her that he had passed away. He asked me to remind her about the pile of feathers she had found, describing the exact location, but more importantly to remind her of the wild hare who had run towards her (despite her calling and searching for the rooster), stopping only feet away, staring into her eyes for a few moments, before turning, running and disappearing into the hedgerow. That was a visit from her dear rooster, trying to reassure her his existence continued, and to waste no more time searching for him.

When one of my own cats, an extremely Zen and loving, handsome, huge ginger tom named Lennox passed away suddenly and unexpectedly in his sleep, my entire family visited a few days later to pay their respects and reminisce about this very special Soul. I always referred to him as my Zen Buddhist in a fur coat and my Homeopathic clients adored him as he comforted and counselled them through their most difficult days. Suddenly, silently, and seemingly from nowhere (our garden is surrounded by very high walls and fences) a very old, very dishevelled looking skinny ginger tom cat appeared. He walked stiffly straight towards the conservatory, which was overflowing with people and had up until that point been extremely noisy. I opened the door for him, and he stepped inside as if he owned the place! He greeted each person there with a cheek rub here, a demand for a stroke there, his tail caressing each pair of legs as he passed among us (very much like Lennox would do). He gratefully accepted the snack and drink offered, then proceeded to take a nap, in the way that cats often do – with one crumpled ear and one rheumy eye on the proceedings; after about an hour, he asked to leave.

It was *way* too soon for us to think about taking on another cat, but I promised this charming yet battered old soldier that if he wanted to, he could have a home with us for however long he wanted; it would be warm, and he'd be well fed and loved. He glanced over his shoulder offering silent thanks as he headed across the lawn, sashaying his ancient stiff hips in the most dignified way he could muster. We never saw or heard him scale the 8ft wall and we never saw him again.

My cat Lucy returned in bee form on the day of her funeral, because she simply had to supervise and ensure everything went according to her very detailed plans! She supervised the 'State Burial' and planting of her chosen rose outdoors, then led us indoors for her Wake, staying until every sandwich and cake had been eaten and every drop of tea consumed from the best china, before taking one more buzzy, stripey, furry butt fly-past and departing out of the open door!

'Bentley, is there anything else you would like me to pass on to your Mum?'

> 'I'll still be around and I will be waiting for you when you cross over and that will be another chapter. It's not good-bye, just au revoir.'

I love being able to pass on the message that our beloved animal friends will be reunited with us once we also return to pure energy. Bentley had already explained that human Spirit and animal Spirit can be in the same place after death (through his connection to the little girl). This simply confirmed my belief that there is no separation from loved ones once we no longer have a living body and, contrary to some belief systems, there is one Heaven, where humans and animals can reside together if they choose. (Some animals, such as wildlife or intensively farmed animals may naturally choose to not share paradise with humans, and who can blame them?) Some people believe that animals don't have Souls and can't go to Heaven, but if they didn't have Souls, I wouldn't be able to contact them, and, if they didn't go to Heaven, I'd want to go where they go!

Bentley approached me, and his Spirit form began rubbing his face against mine; soft, black furry cheeks caressing pale Celtic skin, and he asked me to pass this on to Janet. As he was drawing his energy back and away from mine he asked me to tell Janet that he would be sending a rainbow to remind her of his presence and to make her smile. Rainbows are such strong symbols of hope, light in the darkness, sunshine after the storm, and are often seen as a comforting sign to the bereaved of eventual reconciliation and an end to sadness.

Chapter 3

Not Every Soul is an Angel

Janet: There was some chaos before the start of our third conversation. Bentley's photograph was missing. A frantic phone call from Clare and I rummaged around my own computer files to find the appropriate picture. More haste less speed I have to say. We must have spent ten minutes trying to sort ourselves out.

The first words from Bentley were…

> 'My goodness. What a palaver. I've had great amusement watching you two birds flapping about!'

Over the years Bentley has often used his photograph to play tricks on us – he will hide the printed version, and his digital image will sometimes simply pop up on my screen at inopportune moments, usually to tell me to slow down, stop flapping about some deadline or piece of work I'm preparing, and sometimes just to say 'Hello'!

> 'Despite everything I've said in the past I could be as cute as a button when I wanted to be. Mum could tell just by looking at my face what mood I'd be in. Let me tell you how much I love her. I let that woman ruin my 'street cred' by fussing me and using soft talk in public. But in private I loved the bones of her and would happily pound my paws over her heart as we caught up on the day. Sometimes I would quiver with excitement at simply the sheer joy of living. But I could just as easily roll on to my side

or back and dismiss her when I wanted to, and she was pretty good at knowing when to let me be. Not me though, I would pound over her heart until I got what I wanted!

One day, when her time for transition comes, I will sit on her chest to release her heart so it can join mine. She will not be alone. I'll be there, not the human Spirits. Then I'll run ahead of her to lead the way and show her what it is to be free of restraints. Some human Spirits she knows don't fully appreciate how wonderful it is, but you don't become a Saint automatically on passing over, and not every Soul is an Angel.'

There are some humans in Spirit that Janet has no intention of meeting up with again on the other side, and she was relieved to hear that Bentley hadn't met them and indeed would not be seeking them out. Bentley then showed me some friends he *had* made. A black Scottie dog, a battered ginger tom cat, a Boxer dog with a displaced jaw and a white goat that went by the name of Sammy.

'And always the child of course, Charlotte. I have taken on the persona of the happy cat and it is drawing her out of her shell.'

Bentley showed me an image of a beautiful summer's day in a green meadow strewn with wildflowers, Charlotte lying on her back, holding Bentley aloft above her head as she smiled and giggled with delight, and yes, he did look rather cute!

'See, I'm not always bossy, only when they need it, but Mum's behaving better. She's not off the ciggies but at least she's thought about it. I don't care much for the dancing. Silly clompy feet. Still it makes her smile and it moves her about a bit. I know she's coming to see you, she told me, and then we will see how much self-restraint she has. You do realise she will never really give me a break, don't you?'

Janet: I had indeed been line dancing and by this time I was intrigued by the whole communication thing so had booked myself in for one of Clare's Animal Communication Workshops.

Bentley was confiding in me that he knew once Janet had learned Animal Communication from me, she'd never leave him alone!

> 'Thank her for trusting me and for loving me. She can always rely on me. Tell her the flower beds look better. Remind her about the library books.'

Janet: As ever I pondered on Bentley's words. Yes, I had finally taken myself into the garden and done a bit of work, but my three times a week line dancing sessions had been reduced to 'clompy feet'! And the library books, what was he talking about? Then I spotted it, one library book waiting by the front door to be returned. I went to take a look at it and inside I had left a bookmark. Not any old bookmark, but the only one Bentley would so often play with while I was reading, so it was very special to me. If he had not mentioned the book it would have been returned and the bookmark would have gone forever.

I was also pleased to hear about his new found friends. Bentley had never been one to worry about friendships but I hated the thought of him being on his own. He had always had a strange kind of relationship with Dave, the ginger cat from around the corner, at least strange by human standards. Bentley generally tolerated Dave, but when it became too much he would simply place his head under

Dave's middle, bring his head up with lightning speed and Dave would sail into the air in a vertical take-off motion and then hit the ground running, only to return 20 minutes later from another direction.

Bentley was the Alpha cat of the area, and as I discovered one day when he had gone missing it was a very large area indeed. Knocking on doors to enquire if anyone had seen him I realised he was known by, what seemed to me, half the town's human population. This I thought quite amazing because even if Bentley liked you he'd still ignore you, and if he didn't care a toss about you one way or the other he'd just walk off. I never got around to the rest of the town because he was found accidentally shut in a neighbour's spare bedroom.

If the chips were down though, Bentley and Dave made a grand team. When a new cat moved into the area and took up residence a few doors down from us, this posed a problem for a short time. One night, Bentley had not returned home and at 2am I went in search. I came across Dave (who looked a bit surprised to see me at that time in the morning!), but he continued on his way. I followed. He turned into the front garden belonging to the new cat. I stood at the top of the pathway. There was Bentley. The two cats acknowledged each other and Dave took over Bentley's spot. Bentley, who I feel sure under normal circumstances would have then cut across the other gardens, trotted over to me and the two of us strolled home together. I had witnessed the changing of the guard. This new cat was not going to be allowed to get away with anything!

I first became aware of this rather special relationship between Bentley and Dave when Dave walked through my front door one day because I had left it open. Bentley was indoors so I knew there could be trouble. Outside was one thing, inside something else entirely. I attempted to get rid of Dave by making 'shoo, shoo' noises and flapping my arms around a bit. To my amazement the hackles went up on the backs of *both* cats. The object of their displeasure was me. It was not my job to decide who came and went. My job was to pay bills, provide food and suitable shelter! The two of them walked side by side down the hallway, out through the front door and along the path, tails raised, one black, one ginger. I think I had been ganged up on. I realised I had not only overstepped the mark but was unworthy, and definitely cat enemy number one.

There was also always a routine with human guests to our home. They would be tolerated for a certain length of time, as determined by Bentley. He would then walk into the room, sit down and stare unblinkingly at the visitor(s). Very occasionally someone has been known to withstand this for as long as ten minutes. I would watch as people squirmed in their chairs becoming more and more uneasy, then suddenly it was 'I really must go now'. We would bid our guest(s) farewell; no one ever outstayed their welcome. 'Well done Bentley' I would say with a smile and we would then settle down and relax, just the two of us.

Chapter 4

You Can Choose Your Destiny

Janet: This conversation was mainly discussing my attendance at Clare's weekend workshop on animal communication. I'd had a very enjoyable time there with lots of teachers around including a cat, a chicken and a tortoise who insisted on having a pee at the most inappropriate time. It was all great fun unless the tortoise got you!

I think I did reasonably well and was amazed at how often a picture would enter my mind in answer to a question. Sometimes I found the answer quite unbelievable so I would try to think of the next best thing. I discovered that, however strange, the trick was just to accept the answer because that was the right one. When I tried to analyse something it all went horribly wrong.

Standing in a London Underground train on my journey home from the workshop I spied a Guide Dog, the first animal I had come across post workshop. This was my chance and I had no intention of letting it pass me by. I introduced myself to the dog. I hasten to add this can be a thought process so it was not necessary to make a complete idiot of myself in a crowded train. The dog ignored me. I tried again with no result. Had I blown it already and not taken on board anything I had been taught? For a third time I attempted to strike up a conversation and then got a reply which took me so by surprise. A very loud, gruff, and it has to be said, irritated voice said 'I'm working'. I spluttered my apologies and remained silent for the rest of the journey, but I had done it. I had *communicated!*

Was it any wonder then that Bentley started our fourth chat with the following?

'My Mum expects to run before she can walk. She's a funny old thing as half the time she sets extremely low expectations of herself and the other half she expects to be an expert. But she was so glad to hear from me when she was with you. Well, let's face it, she asked me often enough beforehand to come through and help her! And then again, she's funny – half the time saying I need to be free to do my own thing and the other half asking if I'm still around to help her. From now on she needs to trust her instincts more, and worry less about what other people tell her. She did really well when she met you. I heard you say "No constipated expressions"* and I know she thought that would be her. But she was good, and she tried to not make answers up from her own head.'

*An expression I coined over years of observing students trying too hard to force an answer from the animal from inside their own brains instead of relaxing and letting the messages flow from heart to heart! How often have I seen that strained, almost pained expression associated with trying to forcibly eject a thought or idea from their brains! The furrowed brows, taut jaws and fingers clenched around pens as they strain to come up with an answer to the questions we just asked the animal. And the look of sheer relief when they finally relax, and the answer pops out without even trying!

'Now she needs to refine how she asks the questions and how she interprets the replies. And remind her that everyone is different, so what works for one won't necessarily work for another. She has time to see what works for her. I'm proud of her though, that she tried and didn't feel embarrassed to give her answers. One thing she has to realise is that SHE can choose her destiny to a large extent. SHE can choose who she spends eternity with, and that she will not be judged for choosing animal Spirits before human forms. You deserve to spend eternity with those that make your heart leap and soar and I am number one in that

> category! I'm not being arrogant, just speaking the truth.'

So many animals have reinforced this message; that we get to choose our own afterlife, and who we spend it with, and there's no judgement based on who we do and do not intend to be with. Bliss.

> 'If she trusts me and doesn't try to force the information or interpret it, she won't go far wrong. She's not interested in doing what you do for a living, she mainly did this to talk with ME, so I won't let her down by refusing to talk, even if sometimes I have to say "I'm busy, come back later." She understands that, and she just loves me.
>
> It's funny, she doesn't always believe that she hears from other animals, but she does believe she hears me! I mean, if she can hear ME she can hear THEM. She's new to it and just needs to relax and practice when it's not important to know the answer. Tell her just to make general conversation and not try any hard stuff. Tell Mum if she's trying too hard during the day and gets herself stuck I will come through in her dreams instead so the information is ready for her when she awakes.'

Bentley showed me an image of a giant female snail sitting on the side of one of Janet's plant pots in the garden and suggested that she practice communicating with her 'because she may teach her a lesson or two!'

> 'I've been sleeping on her chest a lot more often as she thinks I need to be physically close to her to be able to hear her and for her to hear me. That's okay, I don't mind really. I even left her some hairs recently.'

> **Janet:** Yes, I had found some black cat fur on my white chest of drawers and yes I do actually do housework, occasionally!

> 'Everything in her life is 50/50 except for me. I am there for her 100%. I love her to bits. She loves me 100%. I am her one constant. With everyone else she never knows what's the truth. Tell her to start writing it down, the things we discuss and the advice I give her because later, when she needs it she won't recall the finer details. And I'm a busy boy, I

don't like repeating myself. I'm not going to nag her about the ciggies anymore. If she won't give them up for me she'll never do it for herself. She has my heart and I have hers and we take good care of them.'

Janet: You would think after the incident with the Guide Dog on the train that I would have learnt my lesson, but Bentley's encouragement urges me on. I talk to dogs tied up outside supermarkets waiting for their human to return with bags full of doggie treats. I talk to cats I come across while walking down a road. Usually, they consider me some form of entertainment which gives them a break from whatever their plans were. Occasionally they follow me, just out of curiosity I suppose. As I worry about them wandering into the path of a stray car, I invariably walk them back after going only a few yards, only to be followed again once I attempt to continue on my way. Luckily cats tend to get bored after a while of just marching to and fro along the pavement and realise it's best to revert to the original plan, before this crazy human came along.

And, just as Bentley foretold, I even befriended a snail and we chatted by my back door for several evenings. I was sitting on the back doorstep watching some very heavy rain, and there was a snail just a few feet away from me. I said 'Hello'.

The reply took me by surprise, 'I'm very wet'.

I said 'But you are a snail, you like the wet'.

The answer came back 'Not this wet!'.

I could hardly believe what I'd heard. I said 'well come up here in the dry with me, I promise I won't hurt you'.

Sure enough the snail started towards me. A kind of confirmation that it was not all my imagination. It took her some time to get to me as it was a long journey for a little snail, but there she eventually was sitting next to me on the step. Oh yes that was much better.

We exchanged a few words and eventually at 10pm I told her I was going to bed but she was very welcome to stay in the dry and we agreed to meet the following evening, same place. Sure enough my snail was there waiting for me the next evening. I joined her on the step. It was still raining. We did not say a lot, just enjoyed each other's company really. This arrangement continued for four evenings and once again we agreed to meet the following night. Evening five, there was no sign of her. I sat and waited but never saw her again. Perhaps she got bored of my limited conversation!

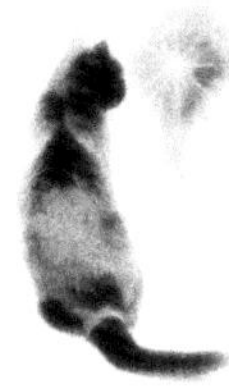

Chapter 5

The Feline Alliance

Prior to each communication session, Janet would email me her questions and comments for Bentley, which I was to deliver on her behalf, and the questions were much like those from most people who had recently lost a beloved animal;

'How are you?' 'Have you visited me lately?' 'What signs do you send to let me know you're around me?' etc.

However, now Janet was a little more familiar with the Animal Communication process, plus Bentley's messages and insights were becoming more revealing and intriguing, she would often ask questions firstly pertaining to things shared in the previous session, and then any updates he'd like to share with us. There's no need to share every response from Bentley (after all most of it is private between two soulmates) so I'll only be sharing the important stuff Bentley wants everyone to know.

'Hi Bentley, it's me again, Clare, your Mum would like an update and to hear anything you would like to share with us.'

> 'I'm feeling rather regal, and important. It seems you think I have the answers to all the mysteries of the Universe, and I'm happy to oblige, but you do understand, it will only be MY perspective, don't you?
>
> I'm on top of the world, where I belong! I always loved to be up high, looking down on the world. You can see things more clearly from up here.'

Bentley showed me a very clear image of himself set against a dark, starry sky, looking down on the Earth below from a lofty height, much like the vision so many of us 'cat people' have witnessed; our feline friends staring down on us haughtily, and often defiantly, from the top of a cupboard or shelf. (Usually one they weren't supposed to climb on...but then, in a cat's mind, nowhere is out of bounds and all things were made for their amusement and entertainment.) It would appear that in Cat Heaven, the sky really is the limit!

> 'Mum, don't run before you can walk with the psychic thing; let those who need to speak come to you. Don't seek them. You have opened the portal by speaking with the animals. You cannot choose who comes through but I will protect you and no bad will come of it.'

Janet: As usual there was a good reason for Bentley's words, although they were not apparent to Clare because I never told her anything about my life.

A few days after the funeral of a good friend, I was sitting quietly in my kitchen, absent-mindedly having a cuppa and looking at the photograph of my friend on the front of her Order of Service. Suddenly her eyes became so bright and alive, they were almost luminous. I stared at them, mesmerised. Then her familiar voice came into my head, so clear and loud.

'I didn't know you could do this.'

'I can't.'

'No, I mean this, talking.'

'I can't, don't do this to me, go away.'

'No, please I want you to take a message.'

'No, don't do this to me.'

'Please, please, you must.'

I was not frightened, how could I be, this was my friend, but the awful thought of having to pass on messages to people who might think I was a crack-pot filled me with dread. My friend shared her messages, only about half of which made any sense to me. I was still saying 'please don't do this to me' when our conversation ended.

I was left with messages I knew I had to pass on but no idea of how to go about it. I held onto the messages for longer than I should have but eventually plucked up the courage to go and see the only two members of my friend's family that I knew. Perhaps they would rush to the phone and dial 999 or physically throw me back out of their front door. So be it, I have no control over what others may think of me. I told them what had happened. They made me a cup of tea and explained what the messages meant to them and perhaps more importantly that they understood them. It was with a great deal of relief that I drank my tea before bidding farewell and strolling home feeling as though a great weight had been lifted from my shoulders.

'Mum listens to my advice, but she closes her ears to some and ignores it! I know I said last time I'd give up going on about the ciggies but I am worried about her if she does not stop. I know she will say she will take her chances but that frustrates and annoys me. I never took stupid chances like that. And I'm not worried about her dying from it and neither is she (because we'll be together again). But, I am worrying about all the things she could endure in life because of it.

My existence will always include her. Why would it not? Yes, I'm busy enjoying myself and learning many wonderful truths but she and I are connected and so therefore my time naturally includes her. I have to keep an eye on her, to stop her from doing anything stupid!'

I need to point out here that in Janet's email prior to every session with Bentley she constantly asked if they'd be reunited, or, she would tell Bentley that if he chose to be somewhere else without her after she passed over, she would be okay with his decision and that he had free will etc., (even though we all knew she'd absolutely hate that scenario!). Occasionally Bentley and I would share a secret eye roll as the question came up once again, and he'd ponder about how to explain it to her in *another* way she might just begin to believe!

> 'Being in this state (in Spirit) is a constant state of relaxation. Everything is a pleasure, a wonder and exciting, but everything is balanced, no melancholy or mania. No stress. The only worries are about those we choose to keep watch over. Does she get it yet?
>
> She thinks she is being sneaky but to me she is transparent. I know what she is trying to find out (about Heaven). Some of it will have to wait until she is here to experience it for herself.
>
> My little girl Charlotte sends Mum a posy of flowers, Anemones and Hellebores. A pretty posy from a pretty girl. I love to see her smile. She has a friend! A human form Spirit. A young boy in blue dungarees. They play barefoot in the meadows. I scamper with them, sometimes leading the way, sometimes following. His name is Peter. They get along grand.'

Here Bentley showed me the sweet bucolic image of young Charlotte in a pretty, floral dress wearing a circlet of blue and pink anemones in her hair, and new boy Peter, in his blue dungarees with the legs rolled up against his bare legs and a white shirt underneath, playfully twirling a daisy between his fingers. They were chasing after Bentley who was bounding like a small deer above the wildflowers in the meadow, black tail aloft and waving ever so slightly in the breeze, leading the children through the fragrant paths towards some new adventure in the sunshine.

Blue anemones represent tranquillity, peace, and inner harmony, while pink anemones represent gentleness, grace, admiration and joy, and are often given as gestures of appreciation or to celebrate new beginnings.

Hellebores represent peace and tranquillity, serenity, resilience and the promise of brighter days. What a beautiful gift from a grateful Spirit child, finally at peace and joyful in her new found companionship.

‘I travel. I have seen places in the world that fascinated me. Thai Temples, Churches perched on cliffs in China and Tibet. Sad Buddhists being oppressed, for what? For loving life and for living their gentle, simple ways. Mum, you must find out what you can on this and do what you can to help. It’s dishonest and it’s injustice to these pure hearts. They are the Spiritual embodiment of Angels on Earth. Their hearts are pure joy and that is what strikes fear in those who would wish them harm – those with dark hearts; for joy conquers their darkness and hatred. Speak out to protect them, but always with joy.

I’ve seen immense beauty and excessive corruption. I’ve seen beautiful Mother Earth being stripped of her beauty and health. Humans need to see it too, before it is too late. I have joined the Alliance, I want to help. I have no ego now. I know Mother Earth needs our collective strength and energy.

We are working to help the Tibetan Buddhists. They hold the secrets of Mother Earth’s joy.’

Here Bentley is referring to a celestial group named the Feline Alliance – Spirit Cats (and some other species) who sit together in Council (like an indigenous circle of Elders), usually at Full Moon, discussing, and helping to resolve ecological issues here on Earth. Their mission is to save Mother Earth and her precious creatures from the foolishness of humans. They drafted me into their ranks many moons ago, after communicating with a rather vociferous and delightful long haired black and white cat named Matilda who introduced me to their work. A self-confessed ‘witch’s familiar,’ with her own magical skills and a voice akin to Almira Gulch (though without the green countenance of the Wicked Witch of the West), Matilda ensured I took my position just on the edge of their circle, where a PA might sit during an important board meeting.

Basically, my job is to sit at Full Moon (usually around midnight) with a journal open and pen poised, taking instruction on prayers, rituals and ceremonies and other ways of helping Mother Earth, and to pass them on to those who understand. But that’s maybe for another book… for now it's enough to know that Bentley had also been drafted into the ranks to help save the Earth.

> 'So, look at me Mum. I'm a campaigner, a do-gooder! Who'd have thought it? Don't get me started on the plight of our tiger brothers and sisters. Starving, tortured. They may decide to leave Earth en-masse if man does not listen to us. Our feline brothers and sisters roar our discontent. Now, I'm busy. I have to help a tiger in a snare. She will survive because we have been protecting her and hiding her young. But, now I must go.'

Oh yes, animals in Spirit can help living animals and as Bentley's story unfolds you will learn the many ways these beautiful Spirit animals are helping and protecting the world's wildlife. Also, when Bentley dismisses you, it's really time to disconnect the telepathic phone call!

> 'Mother, I'll visit you in your dreams when I can. Love you.'

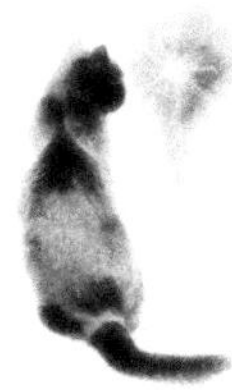

Chapter 6

Extinction is Not an Option

> 'Well, she finally got her act in gear and got into the garden. It's looking a lot more like my garden now. I know I liked to stalk like a panther but the long grass was becoming nasty and the bare soil is a travesty.'

Janet: I had removed a dying hedge leaving a 40-foot border of bare soil.

> 'The colours are finally lovely. I like colour, contrast and variegation. I could have been an artist. It's perfectly fine to use me as her muse to create a restful space and I don't even mind sharing it with Dave, since he makes my Mum smile. But no-one smiles at her the way I did. We shared so many secrets, she and I, but I shan't be sharing any of them or embarrassing either of us at this point.
>
> I am feeling benevolent and loving, and rather proud of my Mum. She has been following my instructions pretty well. Except for the ciggy butts by the plant pots. She is trying I suppose.'

Bentley let out a loud, exasperated sigh like a slowly deflating balloon, then continued,

> 'I've met Bernard, what a jolly nice chap.'

Janet: Bernard was a friend during my teens and twenties. Already in his thirties and a doctor of medicine when we met he seemed terribly old. He became a bit of a father figure in my life and rather kept an eye on me to make sure I behaved myself. Eventually we lost touch, so I was not aware that he had died.

'Charlotte is very happy you like the anemones. If you plant them she will help to tend them. She loves flowers and pretty colours. Peter is practical and brave and loves having someone to take care of and look after. They take care of each other and it is very sweet to see. Charlotte is wearing a ring of flowers in her hair again at the moment. She really is the sweetest child. Her hair is growing long and wavy, getting lighter and it gleams in the sunlight. Peter placed a shiny copper penny in her apron pocket and told her she will never need or want anything again. He's a very kind boy and so thankful you brought the two of them together. Peter says you need a wigwam to grow peas, beans and flowers up. But use string, not plastic, as plastic is bad for Mother Earth.'

Janet: I had just purchased two plastic wigwams and staggered home with them from the local garden centre. They have since resided in the garden shed doing absolutely nothing!

'Now listen, I know I said I was important, well my work is important but I'm not. I'm actually rather humble about the whole thing, now I see how important the work is. I have friends and colleagues who are felines and we get along. We don't have any of the worries or concerns of a physical existence like food, mates, territory etc. so we just get on with Doing and Helping.'

'I'm intrigued, what kind of work do you do, Bentley?'

'I'm a good organiser. I'm efficient. I can see the issue and just get on with it. I'm part of a team and we coordinate and help with the tasks.

We are extremely protective of our feline family and of Mother Earth. We are hiding some creatures away from human sight for now so they can rebuild their numbers. For example the Serval Cat, Bengal Tiger, Flying Fox, Fennec Fox.'

Bentley has explained to me over the years that hiding certain species is a really effective way for the Feline Alliance to protect them from human interference and wrong-doing. Hidden animals can't be poached, hunted, captured for display or entertainment, or used for such folly as 'natural remedies'; for example, rhino horn, elephant tusks, pangolin scales and such 'luxuries' as civet poo (for expensive coffee) and musk glands (for perfumes). The Alliance may also hide animals on the verge of extinction, so to all intents and purposes they appear to have actually gone extinct as far as humans are aware, meanwhile they're healing, rebuilding their numbers and strength, and at a later date they may re-emerge to scientific and global celebration – when they become instantly protected and cherished as they always should have been.

> 'White lions and tigers are a cause célèbre; attention is focused on them while we hide and protect others. Even captive wild ones are helping to raise awareness of the cause. We are softening hearts towards their plight too, unheard of even fifteen years ago.'

This conversation took place back in 2013, and Bentley was referring to the emerging backlash against keeping wildlife captive in zoos, aquaria etc., acknowledging that people were beginning to see that a life in captivity is despicably cruel for creatures such as orcas, dolphins, tigers etc. whose natural instinct is to roam over vast territories.

> 'Don't get downhearted, complete extinction is not an option and together we can restore Mother Earth to support us all. Man's stupidity and arrogance will be his undoing. But even humans will not be extinct. Our business with Man is in his evolution. There will emerge a newer, smarter species not bound by Earthly ties. You are at the forefront and the beginning. Watch the speed of positive progress and let your hearts sing and be glad. Yes Mother, SING!
>
> I'm loving sleeping on your chest at night. Your sleep is less restless now. We sleep heart to heart with an open connection. Your love is my love and my love is your love. We are two parts of one whole.'

Janet: The comments regarding my singing ability are possibly quite justified. As a seven-year-old I had my chance to sing in the school choir – every child got their turn. I was so proud to stand on the stage at assembly and do my stuff. After a few days a teacher informed me I could no longer be a member of the choir because I was making everyone else sing off key!

My Mother was quite horrified by my singing. I had, unfortunately for her, inherited my Dad's vocal cords. That does not mean Dad and I were not appreciated by friends. We were sometimes asked to duet at gatherings, and we were always happy to entertain. Our repertoire included such songs as 'My Old Man Said Follow the Van', 'Does Your Chewing Gum Lose its Flavour on the Bedpost Overnight' and my Dad's favourite, 'Itsy Bitsy Teenie Weenie Yellow Polka-dot Bikini.'

We would sing amid raucous laughter, loud cheering, and much hand clapping.

Generally, I learnt over the years (when attending somewhere singing was required) to just open and close my mouth without making a sound, rather like imitating a goldfish. However, at home I would at times sing with gusto which would bring an 'I want to throttle you' look into Bentley's eyes just before I heard the rattle of the cat flap as he left the premises.

More importantly, and on a separate note, on this occasion the conversation with Bentley through Clare had perhaps revealed answers to some long-standing questions I had. Many years ago, when I was young, I visited a medium, along with a couple of friends, just for a laugh really. During my session a young boy had appeared. He said nothing, just stood there and did not answer any questions. The medium asked if I had any idea who the boy was. I did not.

On three occasions over the years I was questioned by either work colleagues or friends (apparently those more spiritually inclined) about a boy they had seen with me. I could only say I knew of him but add nothing more. Perhaps he was an ancestor who had died young, or someone who had just taken a shine to me. None of this ever worried me, if indeed I even bothered to think about it. Many years later when I consulted several mediums during my initial search for Bentley, the little boy would arrive every time and just stand there, answering no questions, saying nothing. I would explain the situation to the medium and then just say to him 'Hello sweetheart.' I was starting to feel very protective of *my* little boy; after all he had been around for thirty years or so. On one occasion he brought me some flowers, white daisies! Could he and Peter be one and the same?

Chapter 7

Daisy Chains of Love

Janet: By this time, I had a lot of questions to ask and things to say to Bentley. As a human, I wanted him to know how ashamed I felt at the behaviour of my species towards all others.

How wonderful I thought his words were, I thought he could have been a poet.

That as he had left his ego behind I would take care of it for him.

And finally, what was my connection to Peter? How did I bring him and Charlotte together?

> 'Will you please tell Mum thank you for all the nice things she said about me. I know she means them most sincerely and she barely needed to put them into writing because... I KNOW. We never had that kind of relationship where we needed to say things verbally. Our hearts just knew. She's my special girl though, just as I'm her special boy, so there's no more to be said on the matter.'

Janet had apologised for human failings in taking care of the planet and her creatures.

> 'Okay, it's good that you feel shame about what humans have done to the planet, but please know we do not hold either of you directly responsible. We are targeting people like you to help raise awareness and get the information out to a wider audience.

> You're the good guys; the hope.'

While this may sound like an enormous responsibility bestowed upon us, I for one was relieved to not be held personally responsible for any of the dreadful assaults upon the planet and her inhabitants. Give me a job to do any day over being shamed by my behaviour. Throw in a clean conscience and this Catholic schoolgirl is fully armed for the task ahead. This felt better than any Friday night confession!

> 'There is sludge in the oceans and it's beginning to wash ashore on previously untouched lands. That troubles us. Please send healing prayers and light to the oceans to filter out the sludge and to keep the waters clean for our friends who inhabit them. Remember the oceans contribute to the rainfall and ultimately affect the entire planet.'

Whenever Bentley issues a call to action, this is also an invitation to *you* to join us in the prayers and healing. You are invited to join us all in healing and saving our Mother Earth. We *all* have responsibility for her survival, and it's a pretty big job for two women and a small (yet mighty) cat!

> 'Yes, I could see myself as a poet in another life. I'm sensitive, intelligent and an artist, but not like Shelley. I do not suit a ruffled shirt!'

Bentley threw back his head and laughed, and I laughed too, firstly at his feigned indignance, and also because I was starting to see the true character of this mischievous small black cat, and it seemed to me that a ruffled shirt might well be the appropriate frame for this well-spoken, earnest yet humorous, small, black velvet-furred head!

> 'I am happy to be an important part of your life, however to become truly God-like we must let go of ego. I'm happy to shed it, it's not important. You have no need to hold it on my behalf as I do not need it.
>
> Peter and I will explain his story and your connection. Peter has always been with you from many lifetimes ago. You were orphans together in a workhouse. You protected him and when he was big enough he provided

bread for you. Two scruffy urchins who found a spark of light in the darkness and whose hearts are linked together forever.'

Bentley showed me a Dickensian scene of two children, street urchins standing hand in hand outside a large, dark and oppressive building. They were dressed in filthy, ragged clothing, with calloused and grubby feet, bland faces streaked with dirt, and hair unkempt. The eyes of both children seemed huge, set deep into their gaunt, dirty faces, which bore no expression other than resignation. Their ages looked between eight and ten, the girl slightly taller and older than the nervous looking boy. This tragic image of Janet and Peter in their previous incarnation now solved a decades long mystery for Janet.

'I brought Charlotte to you because of my role in taking care of her, another orphan. So, between us, you and I Mum, we were able to provide friendship, companionship and love to two lost and lonely child Spirits. We are all linked heart to heart like flowers in one of Charlotte's daisy chains. Linked, but still individuals. Because of your love for me and your insistence on maintaining contact we have been able to increase our Heart Family. How wonderful is that? We can create our own family based purely on LOVE. The same applies to Bernard. His heart knows your heart, his heart knows my heart. He's a little plumper than in that picture you have of him, and he never grew any more hair. He's well and sends his love.

My work is two-fold; raising awareness with the humans on Earth and helping the animals who are suffering and endangered. More will unfold over time. My Mum's really getting on board with my work, I'm proud of her!'

Janet: The explanation of my relationship with Peter was enlightening and answered quite a few questions for me, not just about the silent boy standing beside me that mediums would speak of. I had been to a workhouse museum a few years before and it filled me with dread. Why? It looked just like my old school, both inside and out. No wonder I hated walking into that school, and to this day I shudder if I walk past one of those old fashioned school buildings.

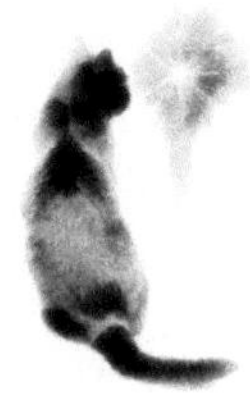

Chapter 8

Pippin

Janet had asked for more information about Peter's story but was told,

> 'Today is not an appropriate time for Peter. His life story is separate from my messages.'

> **Janet:** This was enough to convince me not to pursue the subject. I suspect Bentley knew that I would investigate the two children if I had more information and obviously that is not for me to know. Bentley has a knack for knowing what I'm thinking and answering questions without being asked.

Umm, maybe because he's *telepathic*, Janet?

Bentley wished to explain how and why certain humans on Earth end up helping the animals in Heaven to complete their mission.

> 'It's very easy for us to target our ambassadors. We choose those with genuine love for ALL animals, not just the ones at their hearth. We can see your hearts and we know who is genuine. Sometimes it takes years, decades of work even, until a human is ready to learn about their mission, but we never give up. We send in the 'special ones' (special animals who touch their hearts in ways other animals do not) to raise awareness and vibration levels so they begin the task almost on autopilot; as if it were entirely their own idea. Or we use a mediator such as you Clare to kick start the process. We don't just target single species

people like 'cat people' or 'dog people', oh no; it must extend beyond one species, to a love of ALL species.

We are all ONE SPECIES – because we are all made from starlight – but some people do not see that (yet).

However, there are so many different species, and because humans have free will they are often drawn more towards one species than another. For example, there are those speaking up for the dolphins and cetaceans, those for polar bears or for lions or tigers. This way more is done to save individual species and therefore us ALL. And sometimes we even encourage the poacher to turn gamekeeper if their depth of knowledge will help our cause. There is a reason and a method in everything we do.

Never despair or give in to darker emotions. Keep your energy pure; avoid that which brings up negativity and ugly emotions. Protect your heart. If it feels uncomfortable or wrong, it is.

Our next big mission is raising awareness of all the man-made materials such as plastic bags and containers that are suffocating Mother Earth and her Beloveds (the animals and plants). The seas are already poisoned, the land masses are dumping grounds and our Special Ones (the insects) who are geared up for breaking down and processing waste cannot cope. Mother Earth is crying out for us to help her breathe. Watch and learn as we raise this awareness globally, and YOU can help.

My Mum is loving being an evangelist for Nature, and I love watching and motivating her.'

Janet had one more question for Bentley,

'Is this cat that arrived on my doorstep for me?'

'Of course, I sent this baby to my Mum. How else could it have all ended up this way? My Mum is stronger than she thinks, and she wouldn't ordinarily be hoodwinked so easily! But I knew she would never have gone to a shelter to look for him, and he needs a special heart to nurture him. They will make a wonderful team and she will never regret giving

> him a home.
>
> I call him Pippin, he is so sweet and playful – he is like the playful side of me without the guile and maybe the wisdom, though he does have a wisdom all his own; it's just not that obvious yet because he's been scared and upset. He is no more than 12 months old and he had a hard start in life.
>
> He doesn't really look anything like me, so Mum won't get confused and call him by my name, so she won't reject him as a companion. She's worried she is not good for him, but she IS for him, it was all planned. I will help him settle in and when the time is right, I'll introduce him to all my safe places. My Mum will be a great influence on Pippin, but she MUST heed me on this – NO ciggies near him! His chest is delicate.
>
> There's a secret mission for them. I just want them to be together now. They both have love to share and a strong survival instinct.
>
> Mum has been talking to me a LOT recently, mainly about Pippin, but other stuff too, though she's not been LISTENING too well. She's too stressed out.'

This is something the animals frequently tell me, that their humans talk to them almost continuously, but they never slow down or stop to listen for a response. Whether that is because they don't actually believe animals *do* communicate, (in which case, why are they talking *at* them non-stop?) or they don't believe that *they* can hear them (so why are they torturing their animals by talking and asking questions they fully believe they'll never hear the answers to?) Is it any wonder animals are often confused and feel the need to act out?

Yet *listening* to our animal friends is the easiest and most effective tool we can use in strengthening our relationships.

Try it yourself today. Set some quiet time aside when you won't be interrupted. Send out a wave of love to your animal from your heart, so they feel it and know you sincerely wish to hear them. Ask your animal friend a question; nothing too heavy, (no health or behaviour concerns) and wait for their response. If you hear a word, see an image, feel a physical or emotional sensation that you weren't previously aware of, more than likely you just made a telepathic connection with your pet! Of course there's more to it than this, and there are techniques that can help you connect more easily and deeply, and receive mind blowing and intimate messages of love from your animals, but to Listen With Love™* is the basis of *all* effective interspecies communication.

Yet even some of my best students sometimes struggle to hear their animal's reply if they're too stressed or too invested in the answer, for example when their animal friend is sick, or approaching the end of life. It's not too surprising they forget their abilities and the lessons I've taught them if they put undue pressure on themselves, but the process is exactly the same as always; staying connected to that wave of love and focusing on *listening* to the replies. It's switching the brain off that gets them every time! So sometimes at this stage they may call on me. Being unattached to the responses, I can give them the answers they seek without putting undue pressure on myself.

> 'So, tell my Mum, I don't worry one bit that she might be replacing me with him, because I am IRREPLACEABLE! Pippin does indeed like her, but he's picking up on her negativity and confusion, plus he has the fear she may not let him stay. But now the decision is made, she will calm down and so will he. He has already opened himself up to her and is trying to trust her.
>
> The time is right for her to 'Have A Cat' because our relationship has developed beyond that now, so she can have both without compromise. Plus, she needs someone to kiss who won't object if observed! I'm sending them both the energy of amber for protection and support whenever I'm busy.'

Amber is believed to have properties that heal the nervous system, promote self-confidence, and clear negative energy.

---

* Listen With Love™ is the Animal Communication teaching programme within the Free Spirit Academy™ by Clare Metcalf.

If you're wondering about Bentley sometimes selecting crystals and stones at the end of his sessions, he's not the only one. Many animals tell me about the healing properties of crystals, also herbs, plants, flower essences and remedies. Animals have stayed connected to the Ancient Wisdom that we once all had access to (but humans have forgotten much of this now) and they instinctively know what will heal them and their loved ones. And they love us so much, they want to share their wisdom, to inspire us to tap into the wonderful well of knowledge we once had constant access to. Living more like the animals will help us all live happier, healthier lives.

> **Janet:** Pippin was a mess, not physically (apart from some conjunctivitis and being painfully thin) but he was emotionally broken. When I spoke to him in a separate session via Clare he confided in her…

Pippin: *'So much bad feeling around me, so much negativity and discomfort. Why do I cause humans to be hateful? All my life I felt neglected, rejected and abandoned. All my life I felt like no one wanted me or loved me. I was loved when I was little, cute and playful but I grew*

up with big claws and teeth and I wasn't wanted. I won't let my heart get broken again. What you see is what you get and if you don't like it just stay away from me.

I hate feeling trapped, shut in and confined.

I have so much love to give, I'm never sure whether to hold back, due to constantly being let down. She (Janet) has a kind heart and I don't want to burden her. I like it here, it's very calm usually. She's very calm and never raises her voice to me. She talks to the other cat (Bentley) and says I'll never replace him – as if he'd let me! He put his paw benevolently on my forehead the day I arrived. He told me I was home. Then, I wasn't sure, but now I am. I will try my best to be a good boy and not cause her any upset or sorrow. I'd love to stay if that's okay. She does talk to me a lot, much more than I'm used to but the other cat says I'll learn to zone out when I'm bored.'

Janet: Of course, he could not replace Bentley. He was not Bentley, he was Pippin. The most frightened, damaged little chap I would ever wish to come across. It was one paw forward and two paws back time and time again, but he was brave and without a mean bone in his body and we both knew he would get there in the end.

There was fun and laughter and love. He never got over his fear of people, apart from me. I was not people; but as he once said, 'We get along grand.'

He made friends with other cats too and it gave me great joy to watch him play and chase around with them, finally carefree and happy.

Chapter 9

Sing Your Own Song

Janet: I usually had plenty of questions I wanted to ask Bentley but tried to keep them to a minimum. This time I just said three things:

'Please give everyone my love.'

'Why did my anemone die?'

'Can I have a house in Heaven?'

Bentley, of course, had much more to say.

'My Mum, the Tiger Lady! I like that and I'm proud of her. My Mum's putting her mouth where her heart is. She is speaking up for what she believes in. She's amazing.

Look at me, I'm getting younger. There is a kind of reversed ageing process when you're in Spirit. We go back to perfection, and I don't mean that in an arrogant way. We are all created perfect. It is our choice to maintain perfection or taint it, whether by external influences, poor decision making or, more frequently, not being true to our own story. Not singing our own song. You cannot sing someone else's song and you must not let anyone else attempt to sing yours. You'll only have to go through the process of composing it all over again.

Humans in particular struggle most with this message and create so much difficulty and struggle for themselves and others. There should be no differentiation between sex, or colour, or belief. Animals do not

> differentiate, (except for breeding purposes). Humans are trapped in their own ego. I AM, they say, and then try to create themselves from what they want others to perceive. JUST BE. Care less about how anyone perceives you. That is their business. Be true, be honest, and be real. Be yourself in all your glory because essentially your essence is glorious.
>
> Beauty is everywhere if we choose to see it. The reverse can also apply. What do you choose to see? Step into the beauty and stop wallowing in the negative. From a pure and beautiful perspective everything becomes clear. You need no-one and nothing. All will be provided for you even if you can't see how. That is not for you to question. Believe me; I speak the truth in sincerity. JUST BE TRUE TO YOURSELF.'

Bentley looked at me, and using one paw, feigned wiping sweat from his perfect black velvet brow.

> 'Phew! I just felt I had to say all that.
>
> There is another small awakening happening because the Soul known as the Caged Bird now flies free. Because she now flies free there is a raising of consciousness, there is a new awakening.'

Janet and I believe this refers to Maya Angelou who had died the day before this conversation took place. Maya Angelou grew up in the segregated south (US) and became prominent in the American civil rights movement. A teacher, poet, actor and director, she wrote seven autobiographies including 'I Know Why The Caged Bird Sings.'

> 'People, (humans) listen more to the dead than to their own living hearts. How sad and mystifying. A belief that one can only be a Saint or an Angel following one's death. Not if you remain in your perfection. Earth Angels are everywhere, yet people fear, despise or ridicule them. Once the beating heart has stilled, then they listen, because they are no longer a threat to man's comfort levels. Once they pass there is no expectation to change on their behalf.

> It is time to listen to the Earth Angels in all their forms. Many are not human, for obvious reasons. Almost all are accompanied by, or have an affinity with, animals. The reason should be obvious. We SEE and FEEL the pure Soul, the perfection. We overlook the mistakes and the detours along the way. We understand because we are pure love.'

I adore these insights and snippets of wisdom from Bentley because they make such sense, and they colour everything I do in my own life, in my teaching and in working with animals and humans. I share his wisdom (with Bentley's permission) with anyone who will listen. And they're always fascinated by what he freely shares with them, recognising what an honour it is to learn the wisdom of this special Heavenly resident.

I find it fascinating that humans can often take or leave another human's advice, yet when it comes from their beloved animal they fully embrace the wisdom and tasks they may set for them in order to attain their own perfection.

'But how do they know that?' is the question I'm most often asked.

'How does my rescue dog know that about me?'

'How does my horse know all about the healing properties of crystals?'

'How does my cat know I need to meditate?'

Because they are in touch with Ancient Wisdom, and their own wisdom is not tainted by others who may have hidden agendas.

My advice to students who may discover a 'brilliant book' or follow a 'brilliant spiritual leader' is to remember that they can only speak the truth from their own perspective. It's *their* truth, not Universal Truth. The contrast when animals speak is that they never speak from ego or a need to manipulate. They simply speak the truth. So, you can trust the words that Bentley and the Feline Alliance speak, because it's Universal Truth.

> 'Okay, back to Mum because I know she likes to know what I'm up to. I am being prepared for the Council of Elders. How funny that I am getting younger yet I'm joining the Elders! It's a great honour.
>
> I very much admire the little chap she now shares her life with. (Pippin). He's an open book, full of joy. I'm so proud of her for taking him under her wing and protecting him. They are a perfect match.
>
> I accompany Mum on her talks and presentations. She asks for my help frequently and I will always support her. She's more fired up about her topics, yet more mellow than she has been in ages.'

At this point, Bentley finally addressed Janet's questions.

> 'I will pass on her messages (to the people over here in Spirit) though at this time I have nothing specific in return other than the assurance of their continued love for her.
>
> The anemone was planted in the wrong position, it got crushed and the roots dried out.'

Janet: Seems even Charlotte could not rectify all those negatives.

> 'A house in Heaven? The Soul has no boundaries, no need for such things. I visit OUR house (on Earth) but that is for the Souls who live within it. My Mum is still a crazy nut. I love her totally, completely, honestly and without conditions, just as she does me. She can create her perfect paradise any way she likes, however we have no need for shelter here.'

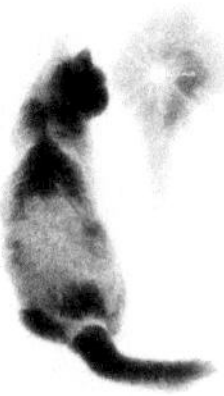

Chapter 10

Of Miracles and Magic

By this stage, both Janet and I were always eager to hear what Bentley was up to in Heaven and what wisdom he was ready to share with us (and the world). I love all my sessions, but Bentley's were becoming a particular treat. Additionally, Janet was asking fewer questions of Bentley, knowing full well that he is telepathic and already knows what she wants information about, and also that Bentley will only answer what Bentley feels is appropriate for her to know at that particular time! As for myself, I'd rarely dare to ask a question or offer an observation, since I was so preoccupied with holding my breath – waiting for the next golden nugget of wisdom.

> 'Please tell my Mum I look younger and younger all the time. I'm absolutely in my prime. She'd be so proud of me.'

Over many years of working with animals in Spirit I've learned that once we arrive in Heaven, we can choose how we will present ourselves to those who can still see us. Occasionally I see older animals and people. As we've already learned, animals and humans can and do meet up, and what better evidence for a client than if I can describe a family member who is taking care of their beloved animal? The older appearance is often the client's lasting memory of them, so they're easy to identify. However, other times they show themselves restored to health and vitality, absolutely in their prime (and often there's a physical photo somewhere of them looking just like how they reveal themselves to me). We don't carry disabilities and infirmities into the next life unless we choose to. And Bentley was certainly looking sharp!

> 'It's strange, I feel like a student beginning this huge game of life, or a youngster eager to learn at the knee of the elders and wise ones. I am being schooled in the way of life, of existence, of miracles and magic. There are no difficulties we can't overcome. No problems are insurmountable. That is all an individual perception. Never doubt there is more going on behind the scenes. They say there's another species of tiger extinct? No, it's purely another species hidden from humans, by us, to gather strength. Then they can decide whether to either re-emerge, or to simply leave the planet for good if humans don't deserve their company.
>
> Mankind does not appreciate our majestic and beautiful gifts, (wildlife) so we are taking them back. It's strange seeing the species that humans fixate on. Pandas have no desire to live on this planet, to be gifted to other humans and to be stared at and their personal instincts interfered with. Bravo to them I say, if they refuse to bring more life into the world. Yet humans waste money, resources and great scientific brains on this. They are unable to prioritise. How we wish to bring them (the pandas) home, but first humans need to realise their folly and release them to make their own choices. Give them the freedom to disappear from a planet that values them in all the wrong ways, or value them for who they are and let them decide their own fate. They know they cannot help this planet and may prefer to leave, but no one will let them.'

This wasn't the first time Bentley had informed us of an active campaign to hide entire species from humans, letting us believe they've gone extinct, enabling the species to decide for themselves if they wanted to regroup and remain, or simply quietly leave for good. So now I no longer become as infuriated at news of a species extinction, instead I check the news and look out for a big pirate wink from my black velvet furred friend in the stars! That's not to say we can become complacent about extinction. It's still a very real threat if mankind doesn't heed these warning shots.

I just like that feeling of belonging to a rather exclusive club, with its vast library of information.

> 'The bees on the other hand are doing stellar work in raising human awareness and consciousness. The irony of it. The small and seemingly insignificant can often make the biggest impact.'

This conversation took place in 2014, around the time people were becoming aware of the vital role bees have on the survival of all life on the planet, and finally people were campaigning against the use of Neonicotinoids in order to protect our precious bees and insect population. Sadly, even now, bees are still not entirely safe, but haven't they done fantastic work informing the general public of their plight?

After blowing our minds somewhat, Bentley finally turned his attention to Janet and her questions.

> 'Charlotte and Peter are so happy; they have accompanied you in the garden and outdoors during this summer of sunshine. They are so happy in each other's company and always grateful to you and me for bringing them together.
>
> Mum, the garden looks beautiful although you still struggle with the anemones. There is a rabbit who wishes to speak to you. Trust yourself, and LISTEN.'

Janet: This was too much of a coincidence. At that time, I just happened to be looking after a rabbit for a neighbour while she was on holiday, so I popped round to have a chat with my furry, floppy eared new-found friend – as you do!

Chapter 11

Pangolins, Giraffes and Carefree Kippers

Janet: In my messages for Bentley via Clare I mentioned again my concerns that Bentley seemed to be working rather a lot with no down time.

> 'Firstly, I'd like you to stop worrying about me. There is nothing to worry about. Here, worry is a foreign concept. In fact, from this vantage point we realise there is never a reason to worry and what a huge waste of energy and resources it is. If I come back to Earthly form sometime, I will be as carefree as a kipper and shall live a totally relaxed and restful life. I do hope I never forget these lessons, and neither should you Mum. If you don't always learn from your own experiences, at least learn from mine. You seem to trust me more than you trust yourself. I love you and I only want what is best for you always.
>
> Now, the tigers are doing well, better than many humans believe but there is always more we can do to help. Raising awareness is only a small part. The people of their homelands must take them to their hearts and treasure them once more. Focus your attention there.'

'How do we do that though, Bentley? We have no access to these people to be able to inspire them to love and care for their majestic wildlife.'

> 'Send prayers and meditate. You can still influence them, even without ever meeting them. Forgive the ignorant and poor; challenge the rich and foolish. Don't back down, be the tigress I know you are. Fight for those in captivity. How DARE humans believe they have the right to imprison animals, our friends, or to decide their fate. One day the balance of power will shift again, but animals don't judge. This world is safer in our paws than in human hands.'

At this stage in our three-way relationship Bentley began to make predictions, warnings, and also to drop cryptic clues about upcoming issues that might impact wildlife and also the planet in general. I began to refer to this as 'our Homework' as there often seemed to be a call to action for one or both of us; petitions, direct action, raising awareness and research. Lots and lots of research!

Still, we have both learned a lot, due to our Heavenly Education from Bentley. As have a few of my clients who were fortunate enough to get in touch with me just as I would be all fired up over some topic Bentley had me fervently researching or campaigning about!

> 'Help the Pangolins. Save them from ignorance and greed. Watch out for the Reticulated Giraffe.'

Note: This conversation took place in early 2015.

There are eight species of Pangolin inhabiting various habitats across Asia and Africa and their individual statuses vary between Vulnerable and Critically Endangered. Sadly they are the most heavily illegally traded mammals in the world.

Pangolins are shy, gentle and slow moving creatures with sweet faces and armoured bodies covered in scales made from keratin. Tens of thousands of them are captured and traded every year and they are being poached to near extinction. They are killed for their meat as well as their scales and body parts, all of which are used in Traditional Chinese and African Medicine.

In the past decade more than one million were illegally caught in the wild and it is estimated that at least one Pangolin is killed every hour in Asia. Research shows that two Asian species of Pangolin could be extinct within the next decade.

However, at the 17th CITES (Convention of International Trade in Endangered Species) conference in September 2016, legislation was put in place to ban the commercial trade of all eight Pangolin species and their body parts.

Reticulated Giraffes were listed as Endangered in 2018 due to a decline in numbers of over 50% during the previous 35 years. This is due to three main factors:

1. Giraffes are relatively easy to shoot and kill and they yield a lot of meat. Plus, there is a growing misguided belief that Giraffe body parts can cure HIV/AIDS, so this has increased poaching exponentially.
2. Habitat loss and fragmentation due to land developments, agriculture or over-grazing.
3. Competition for food and water due to newly introduced species of livestock (the domestic camel) into Giraffe habitat.

It would appear that because little is still known about Giraffe ecology they are rapidly disappearing, but with few people even noticing. The good news is, that thanks to some human efforts (and that of a certain group of animals in Heaven!), their numbers have increased substantially since 2017 in Kenya. Several young Masai have been trained in Giraffe Conservation in Tanzania, (hunter/poacher turned gamekeeper) and Giraffe parts are no longer being used in traditional rituals or as bushmeat. Camera traps are of great use in monitoring the habits and range of the Giraffe and also at helping educate

Northern Kenyan schoolchildren; instilling in them a love for their local wildlife.

Remember Bentley just said that worry was a foreign concept? A waste of energy and resources? Well, he'd just dropped a whole world of worry onto our shoulders, about some species that at the time we were barely aware of! And this continues to be a pattern throughout our relationship. However, I certainly do try to follow Bentley's advice and to send prayers, meditate and send love and healing to every new situation he informs us of. Why not join us?

As we journey through our amazing series of conversations with this wise little cat and he tells us of issues he and his team have concerns about, we often make time to send love and healing up for any of the animals involved to tap into should they choose to. We also hold an intention and energy of love and healing so that any of the perpetrators who wish to change their attitudes, hearts, minds and ways have some vibrational assistance to do so. Our intentions are always for the highest good of all concerned.

> 'Okay Mum, show people they can learn from the past and not repeat their mistakes. And, if you still struggle to meditate, join a mindfulness group either at home or on-line. Be mindful to let go of negativity. Whenever you can, give the benefit of the doubt and send positive energy to difficult situations and personalities. Join a prayer or healing circle.
>
> Charlotte and Peter grow more in love each day; they found bliss when they found each other. They send you a rock rose to brighten the corner of the garden.
>
> Mum, enjoy the summer, I shall try to sit with you in our garden on sunny days and 'help' you like I always did. I'm proud of you. I'm proud that you were my human Mother and I'm proud to be heart mates with you.'

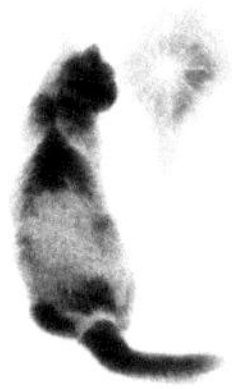

Chapter 12

What Would Bentley Do?

Janet: Once again, I asked Bentley if he ever did anything but work. I also apologised for not managing to deal with his suggestions and the jobs he had given me to do, but that I would continue to try my best. Changing the world however seemed to be completely beyond me. Was I just being a burden? If he needed or wanted me to move aside I would quite understand.

'Mum, why do you have such a downer on yourself thinking you're not worthy of my time, my attention, my love. Of course you are, but I am not going to massage your ego either. Don't feel the need to push me away or 'give me my freedom to do what I need to do'. I am perfectly capable of that, with or without your permission.

Have I made it sound like Heaven is a workplace or a treadmill? That was never my intention. Look at the children, constantly playing in the sunshine. Remember I met them in a sunny field, and we all played together.

Time is different here; there is all the time in the world. There is some urgency with working to save the Earth and her creatures because humans are so stupid and self-destructive, but I spend plenty of time basking in the sunshine, warming my tummy and I also have quiet time gazing at the moon.

I thought you were primarily interested in my work and the important matters that occupy me. I didn't think you needed to know about my downtime as well. Remember I'm in a state of perfection. 100% work makes no one perfect. Everything is balanced. I still play like a kitten at times; we all need balance.

Ultimately, I have no control over your life or how you choose to live it. All I can do is to pass on my concerns for your health and wellbeing because I love and care about you. If you choose to ignore me that is up to you; I'm not living your life for you. But I won't leave you just because you don't always listen to me. I don't get angry or too frustrated with you. It's your journey.

Don't over-analyse my words. Take them at face value and remember I have a sense of humour too. Remember, balance, in all things. Sometimes I just like to tease you, to stop you taking everything so seriously.

Your intuition with Pippin is generally sound and he's cleverer than you sometimes give him credit for. Of course, he's not me but he's no imbecile either. He and his friend are partners in crime. Sure, they'll get each other into trouble sometimes but they'll get each other out of it too. It's his life path. He's a good navigator and he uses the moon and stars well.

Your life is busy but not always with essentials. Don't distract from your life, enhance it.

Even Bernard has his fun side and no, he's not in the lab constantly. He goes driving in an open topped vintage sports car and he goes for picnics to the countryside. He doesn't NEED it for transportation, he has it because he loves cars!'

Bentley had told us that Bernard was excited to be continuing his research in Heaven because it brought him such joy and hope for the future of mankind and animals, because, well, who knows if or when he too could reincarnate and change the world?

Janet: Bernard did always love his cars! And I loved hearing Clare

> describe the image of him driving through a village, waving to all his friends, like a Heavenly Noddy waving to all in Toytown!

It's true, to this day, whenever I recall this conversation I see Bernard, in a shiny bright red open topped sports car, waving to his friends and neighbours who all wave back, delighted to see him, just like a scene from the old Noddy cartoons!

Animals often show me things in my own frame of reference so I understand them, and to help me describe them to my clients, and this one had Janet and I both in stitches, yet she instantly recognised that this would be Bernard's transport of choice.

> 'I'm happy to advise you always but there are some things you just have to work out for yourself. This is your life journey. I'm on my own journey. What's right and appropriate for my evolution may not be right for you. It does not mean we won't meet up again, just that you have your own lessons to learn.
>
> You need to feel things for yourself, experience things for yourself. Enjoy life without second guessing "What would Bentley do?" Remember I'm not perfect, I have flaws too. This is not a criticism nor is it me saying leave me alone and give me some peace. Don't take it that way. I say it with love. Life is for living every second and squeezing every drop out of it like a sponge.
>
> I know you value my advice and wisdom; I appreciate that but don't negate your own inner wisdom and intuition by relying too much on someone else's advice.
>
> My theme today has been balance, and I want you to be careful and pay attention as I don't want you to stumble. You're not too stubborn to listen to me on this one, are you?
>
> I'm working with many species. A rare zebra (Bentley showed me a young zebra with brown stripes), Przewalski's horse, and a rare ass, the Onager. We have to bring them back, to strengthen the gene pools diluted by humans' selective breeding and hunting habits.'

After hearing about these animals from Bentley I did a little research and found the following information:-

Grevy's Zebra is the largest of the wild zebra and born with reddish-brown stripes. They are actually more related to the wild ass than the horse (Plains Zebra are more related to the horse). They have undergone the most substantial reductions in habitat and range than any other African mammal. Due to overgrazing and water shortages, their juveniles have a low survival rate, and research showed that in a 30 year period the population became reduced by around 50%. As a result they ended up on the Red List as Endangered. However, in recent years conservationists are using more technology such as GPS collars to monitor their movement, and employing locals as wildlife scouts to protect them.

Przewalski's Horse was once considered extinct in the wild having been hunted to extinction in the 1960s, but thanks to the discovery of a few wild individuals, plus reintroduction from captive breeding programmes, they are now classed as Endangered in their native Mongolia and China. They are believed to be the last truly wild horse, with DNA studies linking them with an ancestor around 500,000 years ago.

The Onager, also known as the Persian Wild Ass, is Critically Endangered, its numbers have been rapidly declining over the past 50 years due to habitat loss and indirect conflict with human activities. There is a recent study focussing on their migratory patterns and possible poaching habits in an attempt to offer protection and ensure survival of the species.

> 'I love my work; it's certainly not a chore. That's the secret, it's not work when you love what you do. Lighten up and do more of what you love. Forget the rest, it's irrelevant. Only focus on what you love. I do.'

Janet: Well, of course I was, and still am, interested in Bentley's work, but it is nice to know about his downtime too. As he says it is all about balance.

For some reason it reminded me of a time when I had agreed to spend the night at a friend's home after she'd had a medical procedure. I could hardly refuse but wondered how Bentley would feel about me going missing for a night. I need not have worried. Having explained to him about it, the answer was simple. He came too. He joined me of his own accord by following me. There I was in a put-up bed in the living room; not the most comfortable thing I have ever slept on to be honest. Bentley took the easy chair, simply curled up and kept me company for the night. He realised I had a job to do and he was going to help me do it. I have to say he slept a lot better than I did and he did not stir until 5:30 the following morning when he asked to go out. We met up again back home.

That is balance, friendship and love working together.

There was, however, one very memorable un-busy day on 10 August 2003 when the temperature topped 100 Fahrenheit. The garden has a certain amount of shade from trees and I sat on the patio with my feet up reading a book. Bentley was crashed out on the lawn. A toad hung out over the edge of the pond with his back legs dangling in the water to keep cool. There, the three of us stayed for hours. For me it was a very fine day indeed.

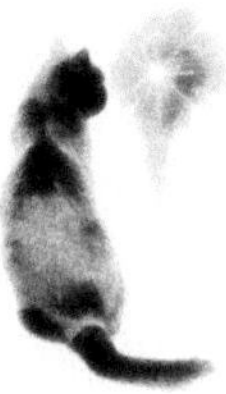

Chapter 13

Collecting Dreams in a Basket

Janet: I asked Bentley whether he had a house or home as I truly felt that a home was very important (and more useful than the vintage car as owned by Bernard) and I pointed that out to Bentley. I also asked him about any particular friends he has. As usual, he began with what was most important to him!

> 'There will be a very special moon tonight; a time to make wishes, set your intentions for the months ahead and ask for help with tasks you want to complete but lack motivation for, or anything that seems impossible. Take a glass or crystal bowl, write the wishes or intentions on paper and place underneath the bowl. Fill the bowl with water and place it in the moonlight.
>
> The moon does influence and govern you more than you realise, not through magic but by magnetism and biophysics. Everything has an explanation; some people seek too hard to find one, and some refuse to believe. It's an individual choice, but the middle ground of just KNOWING is the road of peace, understanding and wisdom.
>
> So, tonight I will be busy, collecting dreams and wishes in a little basket and delivering them safely.'

The image of the sleek little velvety-black cat with a wicker basket over his front paw as he collected these special intentions to be granted still stays with me. This conversation began a routine of

Bentley being extremely busy around Full Moon, so much so that he eventually asked us to not contact him around that time!

This conversation took place on 2nd April 2016 which turned out to be a Libra Full Moon, and a Pink Moon no less!

> 'You ask about houses again, yet you confirm I am a free spirit. A free spirit has no need for boundaries or a place to 'belong' – I belong everywhere.
>
> But this Heavenly state is a matter of choice. What is Heaven for me may not be Heavenly for others. Perhaps if you had been homeless on Earth, a house may be your version of Heaven? And if you lived in a concrete jungle of buildings maybe Heaven would be a cabin in the woods? It's an individual choice.
>
> Bernard has a car because he loved his cars. He doesn't NEED it for transportation, he just loves it. He doesn't LIVE in it you understand, he just enjoys travelling around in it.

The children feel free and happy and safe in the sunshine in the meadows, and because we are kindred Spirits that's how we met, remember?

There's a beautiful white horse with blue eyes in the meadow now, with a long mane to the ground, like rippled silk. To the children she looks like a Unicorn, but she's more likely a winged horse like Pegasus. The children feed her perfect, shiny red apples.

You want to know if I have lots of kitty friends to play with, but I was never that interested in feline hierarchy on Earth. I have one good friend, a striped tabby with a smiley face who is not brown or ginger but almost red (auburn colour). This cat is as cheeky and bold and free spirited as I am. Membership of the Feline Alliance does not mean having to spend all my time in the company of cats. We come together for gatherings such as the Full Moon, during volcanic eruptions and earthquakes. The rest of the time we have our own tasks and of course our free time too.

Right, I'm going to play now before I have to work tonight.'

And with that, I was summarily dismissed!

Janet: It was definitely in Bentley's nature to be a busy cat. Some of it was of course weather dependent. If it was raining outside the front door, was it necessarily raining outside the back door? I was happy to check with him, after all, rain has to fizzle out somewhere, but never it seemed in our back garden.

He had three options; stay indoors, head for the trees or curl up on the garden chair placed just by the back door in the dry under the overhang. I had put the chair there before Bentley's arrival but suddenly there seemed to be an invisible sign above it, 'reserved for Bentley'. Sometimes he would curl up and sleep on it when it was wet outside and sometimes I would sit next to him on the back door-step. There is something very soothing about sitting watching the rain.

I still do it and there still seems to be that invisible 'reserved for Bentley' sign above the chair, and sometimes the back-door step is a very comfortable place to be.

On mornings when he requested a double helping of breakfast I knew something big was going on and that I would not see him for the rest of the day. I would wave him off and tell him to take care. I was never privy to his agendas. Sometimes I would spot him trotting along earnestly, head forward looking neither to the right nor the left, busy going somewhere on an important mission. The important mission of course may have been heading for one of his favourite places to curl up, nap and soak up the sun. Who knows?

Usually, Bentley smelt of wonderful fresh air, rather like a spring day after the rain. I say 'usually' as he did have a liking for next door's compost heap and was known to spend considerable time relaxing on it. Gone would be the aroma of fresh air; instead, clinging to his fur, the smell of… well… rotting compost. Earthy, rich, ripe, *stinky*!

There also seemed to be something about the time of 11:30pm. If he was in, he tended to go out at that time, or if he was out, he tended to come in at that time. I never fathomed out why.

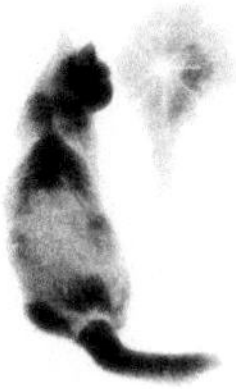

Chapter 14

Of Plants and Planets

Janet: Naturally I had some questions based upon the previous conversation and asked Bentley if he was teasing me – horses with wings?

We had also heard about the discovery of a new planet, could he tell us anything about it?

'Mum, how could you possibly doubt anything I tell you?'

Bentley looked at me with huge, innocent eyes… that just screamed a lack of innocence at the same time! But what he said next convinced me he was indeed earnest in his exclamation.

'Did I invent rainbows? Did I invent stars? I can't invent creatures either. How do YOU know what exists and what doesn't? Have you been to all four corners of the Earth? No, because there aren't any!'

Bentley winked at me and grinned at his own joke.

'I digress. Of course there are horses with wings. There are tiny horses that can swim but can't walk and you believe in them because you have seen evidence of them (seahorses). Well, I have seen creatures you only thought were mythical. Where do you think myths come from? Some might say Witches and Angels and Fairies are mythical, but WE know they are not. I might tease you about your life choices sometimes dear one, but I'd never LIE to you.

You ask me if I have company? I have the children of course and their new equine friend. Is that easier for you to digest?'

Here, Bentley gave me a huge, conspiratorial wink.

'And also, dear eccentric Bernard, driving around with his car roof down, waving joyously to everyone in his downtime.'

Once again Bentley showed me that image of Bernard in his car, roof down, wearing a cravat and driving through a small, pretty village and waving to everyone.

'Company is everywhere if that is what you seek. Here (in Heaven) we are all friends, and the atmosphere is pure love – because here the ego does not exist. Absence of ego equals pure love and joy and peace. No one NEEDS anyone else, but everyone helps when they feel like it – for the joy of it, and no-one WANTS anything from anyone either; it's such freedom.

So, humans have been making our work more difficult again. I wish I could simply remove the ego from every one of them. But there are lessons to be learned from this period of uncertainty. What I AM certain of is that everything works out as it's meant to, so why waste energy worrying and arguing over it? Best to get on with your OWN business because that is all you have any semblance of control over after all. Set a good example and be a good influence. Everything else is personal choice.

Mars and Orion are in juxtaposition causing an unsettled atmosphere and black storms. That's okay, it clears the atmosphere, but it's very unsettling while it happens. There will be more solar flares. Don't believe the scaremongers about them. They are burning off radiation, but Earth becomes aware of them because of the thinness of the atmosphere in places. Don't you want to get rid of harmful radiation?'

This conversation took place in 2016 and prior to publication in 2024 there had been unprecedented solar activity. Solar waves, solar flares and multiple geomagnetic storms, causing the first ever UK wide appearance of the Northern Lights.

> 'There are no 'new planets', only those that have been hidden, like the animals I've told you about. If humans knew the full extent of everything that exists their minds would be blown! Plus, what they don't know they can't destroy.
>
> I want to talk about the Plant Kingdom. They give up everything to sustain life on this Earth; they are completely ego-free. Plants are the most selfless Souls and very few people thank or praise them. Instead, some humans try to replace them chemically, not realising the magic that is in every selfless cell. It's a synergy. The magic does not exist separate from the host.
>
> Our poor Nature Spirits work so hard and fight huge battles to preserve Nature as she should be. EVERYONE should be thanking them daily. Every time you smell a flower or admire a green field or the colours in the trees give thanks to their ego-less Souls and to the Spirits who take care of them.
>
> The children are playing happily in flower-filled fields – they do love tall daisies and poppies to play in – they have a puppy to play with, a 'Heaven orphan' like themselves (a youngster who arrives in Heaven before their parents), whose heart is filled with joy to have the children's innocent playful hearts to welcome him.
>
> Mum we all send our love and there's no homework for you this time, other than what entices you, and of course giving thanks for Nature's glory. I love you so much, you make me proud.'

Janet: I certainly make sure I talk to plants now and tell them how beautiful they are. One day while keeping an eye on a neighbour's property while they were on holiday, we watched a tree fall in their garden. Me standing, Bentley sitting next to me. It was a long thin tree with what turned out to be very shallow roots. What is it they say? 'If a tree falls in a forest and no one is around to hear it, does it make a sound?' Well, we were not in a forest, and we were around to watch it fall, gently, gracefully, and silently. I felt sad to see the end of this tree but as soon as it hit the ground, we were both there clambering over it. Climbing a tree together while still on terra firma. Such fun!

As Bentley was drawing his energy away he waved to me and appeared to be surrounded by deep mauve and purple swirling colours. I asked him where he was.

'I'm in Andromeda Galaxy, with Archangel Gabriel.'

Scientists currently tell us that Andromeda, a spiral galaxy, is the nearest galaxy to the Milky Way and is about 2.5 million light years from Earth. In dark skies you can see Andromeda from Earth even without a telescope, by looking towards the constellation Cassiopeia, (the 'W' shape of stars) which points directly towards Andromeda. And guess what? You can use the Great Square of Pegasus (The Winged Horse no less) to help you locate Andromeda! (An online search will help you locate them all.)

I already had an awareness that felines originated from Andromeda, having had previous conversations with other cats and other cat people. My dear, delightfully eccentric yet incredibly clever friend Dominique Lefort, the famous Cat Man of Key West would playfully hold one of his beautiful feline friends aloft, dancing some imaginary pas de deux while drawling melodiously in his thick Parisian accent, "We are from Andromedaaaaaaa" as human and cat locked eyes conspiratorially in their secret reminiscing. To now see Bentley sitting there at the centre of its swirling colours was an incredible confirmation.

Gabriel is one of the higher-ranking Archangels and is known as God's Messenger. His role is of communicator and messenger of the highest order. He carries your messages to Heaven to those in Spirit and can relay their messages back to you. It doesn't surprise me that he chooses to spend time with a special (trainee higher ranking) cat who also loves to relay messages to and from Heaven!

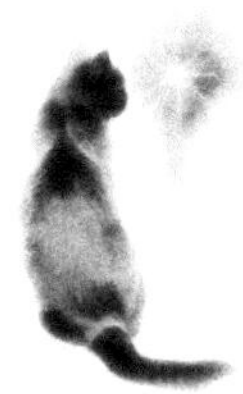

Chapter 15

Blue Footed Boobies

Janet: In my notes for Clare prior to this session I apologised to Bentley for doubting his word in past messages.

I suggested the world might be a better place without humans, based on what a horrible mess we were making of everything, and I told Bentley how proud I am of him for everything he has achieved without help from anyone.

I also mentioned that I had read somewhere that different species can't stay together in Heaven.

'Firstly, you have nothing to apologise for, especially for lacking in knowledge, which is the reason why I remain connected to you; to educate you in matters you are unfamiliar with. Only apologise if you hear my words, but fail to engage in what I tell you, or disregard my words, which, for the most part, I know you are too afraid to do!

You say we should keep humans out of the way with regard to changing the world. But the world will ONLY change by imprinting on and changing them, don't you see? Unless you prefer total species extinction? We ALL have a place here and a role. There is a place for education, forgiveness, understanding and brotherhood. We are all parts of a greater whole.

So, when you say I have achieved much and by myself, well, that's all any of us can do ultimately, as a PART of that greater whole. We have free will in whatever we choose to do with the resources we are given.

Life and existence are precious gifts and to be cherished. It would be ungrateful to achieve anything less than our true potential. It would be churlish even. SEE your potential and reach for it.

Remember I would not choose to remain in contact with you if you were not worth the effort. I am rather busy as you continue to remind me. I CHOOSE to remain in contact with you to continue to educate and encourage you. Haven't you worked that out yet? I don't share all this just because you're inquisitive and constantly ask me questions, that's not my style! I share because it's important you understand it, and also because I know both of you can share this wisdom, not just keep it to yourselves.'

Bentley turned his attention to me,

'I love you dear girl. You keep the records of my words. YOU can make sure my teachings are heard far and wide. Why else did I put you two together? Why? Because you are my scribes. Because paws can only play with pens, not hold them – my little joke.'

As he chuckled at his own joke, Bentley revealed an image of himself in pure cat form, playing with pens in his soft black paws and sending them skittering across a desktop! In contrast, I sit here at every session with notepad and pen in hand, hanging onto his every word, inflection and nuance, for all the world a PA to his exalted executive (stellar) role!

'Now then, you continue to worry about and misunderstand what happens when we leave our bodies. Let me explain (again) about what happens when you arrive in Heaven. I AM NOT A CAT, you will not be a human. We will carry all of the memories, lessons and Spiritual developments of each lifetime, BUT when we leave our physical bodies each time we return to pure energy. You will be pure energy just as I am.

Therefore, we ARE the same, do you understand? So there can be no separate areas for different species because we no longer wear those uniforms. And what draws us together is our resonance, our magnetic pull, our unique heart song if you like. We recognise each other. Every creature that ever had a physical existence returns to pure energy. The

> atmosphere would be most crowded if we all retained physical form. We have a means of locating each other and staying connected and we can see, via our memory, how we were when we were together in physical form.
>
> We can create the meadow, the car or the lab in our imaginations, be and do whatever feels good to our Souls, and that is why this existence is called Heaven because it's the best place you can conjure up in your imagination. It's filled with only those we love and choose to remain connected with. No hate or misunderstanding or sorrow – is that not Heaven?'

Bentley is confirming what hundreds of animals in Spirit have told me time and again, that we recognise each other in Heaven by our 'heart resonance' which is unique to each of us.

When explaining to humans who haven't been blessed to see what has been revealed to me, I describe it like this: our heart is like a magnet, and every person or animal we have ever loved becomes like iron filings. When we arrive in Heaven, that magnetic force (from our heart) sends waves throughout the Universe telling all our loved ones we have arrived and so they gravitate to us like those iron filings would to a magnet. Then our memories recognise each individual heart resonance in the way we remember them best. (So they will all appear before us as the people or animals we knew and loved in life.) It's beautiful, and it ensures we meet everyone we hope to reunite with on 'the Other Side'.

> 'I'm not going to give you much work to do right now because you're busy, but I am serious about getting my messages out to a wider audience. It will be a collaborative effort. I need to not just be special to you two you know... we could call it, "Conversations with Bentley".'

Once again Bentley threw me one of his pirate smiles that always delighted me and at the same time made my heart sink because I knew he had mischief (and more work for me) up his sleeve. I had no idea how much work was about to land on my plate! And yes, cats really do smile and have all manner of expressions, and Bentley's are by far the most expressive, theatrical and effective!

'Everyone here is fine. I know you want to know, even if you didn't 'officially' ask. They send love as always. But my focus is on my messages, especially of life after leaving one's physical body. It's important to know it's not just nothingness or a black hole. It's light, bright, hope and joy. It is nothing to fear or dread because it's a welcome break or respite from the business of physical existence, especially for those who return time and again.

I'm pretty sure I will be here until you arrive so I can keep you on your toes and make sure you're following my suggestions, besides which I wouldn't dare move on or you'd never forgive me!

I want to bring the Galapagos to your attention now because we're celebrating brighter days for some species there. Galapagos is sacred land and must be preserved. It's where we hide many of the species we are saving. The caretakers of those species are the huge Blue Footed Booby birds. They are NOT what you're used to seeing. They truly exist and they take care of the endangered species we entrust to them.

My darling girl, I tell you about species and places as my proof to you that I speak the truth. Not many others will care a jot about proof or evidence, they just want a good read, but you needed to see just how much I know so you could take it all on board.'

Janet: Clare and I were both stunned. Was Bentley actually talking about a book? We had more questions than answers as Bentley was bringing more than his usual level of crypticness!

Bentley knew that I *did* care about proof and evidence. When you do what I have done for so many years, it becomes important to provide solid evidence to bring comfort and help to humans about their animals, and as proof for non-believers. Little did I know at this point, exactly how much research it would involve when proving Bentley's words for his book!

The Blue Footed Booby is a large, distinctive marine bird with brown plumage on its head, a white rump and black tail, and very large distinctive turquoise blue feet. The level of blueness indicates overall health and suitability to mate.

In the 1960s, the Galapagos Islands were home to almost half of the world's breeding population of Blue Footed Boobies; with around 20,000 breeding birds. Sadly, research suggests that by 2012 their population had shrunk to an estimated 6,400 birds, mainly caused by the decline in their preferred food such as sardines, which the Boobies seem to need in large quantities in order to breed. They are also affected by increasing marine plastic pollution. As a result of their dramatic decline in numbers, conservation efforts are now being made in the form of studies, research and attempts to reduce the amounts of marine plastic pollution, (something Bentley already referenced as essential) which can only be good for all marine life (and ultimately all life).

So, in essence, Bentley was telling us we must fight to save the Blue Footed Boobies, because they are the chosen caretakers of all the hidden species that the Feline Alliance are trying so hard to bring back from the brink of extinction. If the Galapagos continues to be tainted by pollution and over-fishing, the Boobies go extinct, closely followed by all the other creatures they protect.

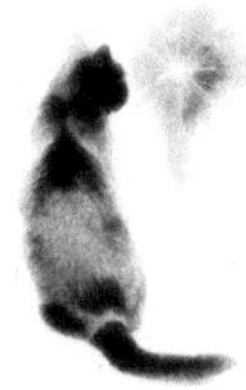

Chapter 16

No Sadness or Regret

Janet: Despite all of Bentley's teachings I was still confused, so I asked Bentley to explain why he stated he was not a cat now but in the past had said he was getting younger and had been restored to his former glory – teeth intact, claws like razor blades etc.

Once again I said that if he needed or wanted to move on not to consider me and that I will forgive him anything just as long as he is happy.

'I'm going to set some confusions straight first of all.

When we first spoke close to my transition I knew you needed concrete evidence it was me speaking with you. You had no idea back then how our relationship and conversations were to develop, and you may not have believed me at that time. You needed to hear from BENTLEY CAT not BENTLEY SOUL, because I am so much more than the cat you knew and still love. So, I spoke as BENTLEY CAT, your companion and friend. I knew we had bigger plans, but you weren't ready to hear them then.

You were grieving and, well, you were a little confused. (Nothing new there then!) So, I was gentle with you and responded as the companion you were expecting to hear from. Likewise, when the time comes and we meet again I may well resemble the physical form I inhabited in our lifetime together so you can recognise me and trust it is me. BUT it is our hearts and souls that will recognise each other.

Eventually we don't need the physical body to recognise each other. However, when I need to tell you about a Soul Friend I have encountered, or need to carry a message from, I need to be able to describe them to you in a 'physical' form that you will recognise, so sometimes I show Clare images of them to make her descriptions of them pretty accurate for you.

As for my getting younger, remember there is no sadness here, or regret, so if you were to arrive to the sight of an old and 'inadequate image of my former glory', it could make you sad. You will have enough to deal with adjusting to your new reality at first, besides which I would NEVER want to be represented as old, sick or frail. But it's mainly about helping you feel better about my departure.

I don't want to hear you disparaging yourself any longer. You are perfect as you are if you just accept yourself.

You must take matters into your own hands and take responsibility for your own health. Trust your gut instinct and also trust me. We are not due to be reunited yet, but some of that responsibility is yours and yours alone. And it's because you're not here that I felt unsure where I was due to be. I don't plan to go anywhere but sometimes we're given important jobs and sometimes we are reincarnated, or evolve, so I can't make any fixed plans. But it's my will and intention to be right there guiding you to our mutual friends when you arrive, and I WILL be the one to bring you home.

Pippin has to follow his own life path. You are assigned to take care of his physical needs, but he must learn his own lessons; no-one else can do that for him. Would you have him return to learn that all over again?

No-one receives their lessons in exactly the same way. If they didn't learn from it last time, there is no guarantee they will learn it next time. It will be the same lesson or message but with a different story attached. For example, if someone has fear in this lifetime there is no point forcing the same fear on them next time around. They need to learn their bravery from a new situation that doesn't make them freeze before it even unfolds.

> But I have explained it in a very simplistic way. I will ponder if you need to know that in some deeper way. For now it's enough to know that if one perceives this life to be a trial, then the next one will have similar lessons but different obstacles in order to clear any blocks that exist to prevent learning, healing and progressing. And if you don't relish that thought then deal with your issues honestly now. It sounds simple, 'just like that!' and in many ways it is. However, some people only realise that when they encounter the same kind of shit time and time again.'

Bentley rarely swore, but I'm sure he chose this word for emphasis, and I wasn't about to ask him about it or correct his language!

> 'There are big changes afoot for wildlife, especially those supposedly under the care of humans. The balance of power will shift and animals will have more rights, not taken by force, but the scales are beginning to lift from mankind's eyes'.

As Bentley's energy was leaving the conversation, he told me that he was sending Janet a big bunch of multi-coloured freesias for a special occasion and a bunch of anemones from the children (psychically of course as Spirit sadly doesn't have an account with a florist!).

Unbeknown to me, Janet was about to celebrate a big birthday, so this was yet another perfect message from her beloved Bentley!

Freesias are said to represent innocence and friendship, and were the ultimate symbol of trust for the Victorians. They also represent thoughtfulness and high spirits which makes them the perfect choice to send to a friend or mother on her birthday!

This conversation took place in 2017 and interestingly since then, many countries have moved towards the acceptance that animals are sentient beings and deserve their own protection. The UK passed the Animal Welfare (Sentience) Act in April 2022. France was an early pioneer for animal protection, designating some animals as sentient beings in their 1976 Law on the Protection of Nature, progressing with the French Civil Code in 2015 categorising animals from 'moveable property' to 'living beings gifted with sentience'. New Zealand, Peru, Sweden and Spain now all recognise animals as sentient beings, and many more countries look set to follow.

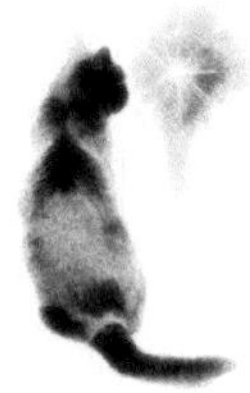

Chapter 17

Feel the Joy!

Janet: This time I wanted to ask Bentley the following:

You say sometimes souls are given important jobs and sometimes reincarnated, or evolve, so you can't make any plans for the future. Do you have no say in the matter? What exactly do *you* mean by evolve?

You said you knew we had bigger plans, so was all this meant to be?

As usual, Bentley answered at his own pace and in his own unique manner!

'Today I'm feeling young and playful. We shouldn't always take ourselves seriously and get caught up and immersed totally in solemn matters. True, my messages are always serious and sincere but we need to be well rounded individuals with humour and downtime and pleasurable pursuits. For me being out in nature and observing all her creatures was a source of inspiration and pure joy. I want you to feel that joy too. I want your heart to be light. I know that many of my messages and the tasks I set you weigh heavy on your shoulders and your mind. I want you to have balance. Light for the shade, joy for the anguish and solace for the pain.

We have been celebrating here; many successes and much joy.

The Fennec Foxes we are hiding are multiplying nicely.

> Wild Chimpanzees are celebrating the release of some of their captive cousins.'

According to our research, in 2015 all Chimpanzees (both wild and captive) were listed as Endangered under the Endangered Species Act (ESA), and in November of that year the US National Institute of Health announced an end to funding invasive Chimpanzee research and would retire all government-owned Chimpanzees. At that time almost 700 Chimpanzees needed to be rehomed from their research centre, so an agreement was made to begin releasing them. Their new home would be a former gorilla sanctuary; a 236 acre forest in the Blue Ridge Mountains in Georgia.

In 2016 the first residents arrived. The releases continued over many years, integrating small groups gradually. Social groups could be kept together to ease the transition, ensuring successful integration as the chimps headed for their well-deserved retirement in peace and in Nature – not quite where they belonged, but a far cry from a government lab.

Also in 2016, the famous Joe, a Chimp who had lived in solitary confinement for 17 years, was finally released to the same centre, where he went on to have his own social group at last.

> 'New cubs have been born to the Tigers of Ranthambore (National Park, India.) They are Royal children. What joy! We all love babies.'

Ranthambore, a former royal hunting ground, was declared as a tiger reserve in 1974 after a census the previous year highlighted the stark reality that there were only 1,827 Bengal Tigers remaining in the whole of India. Hunting of tigers became illegal too, with a high penalty for hunters and poachers. Hunting wasn't their only survival issue though; habitat loss, human encroachment and the usual conflicts with humans over grazing animals made tigers a target for hunters and poachers alike.

A project was set up in India where protected areas for tigers with buffer zones were created. Since the project began, tiger numbers have risen gradually.

> 'Dragonfly and Damselfly numbers are on the increase, also Jays. We have so much to celebrate.'

Dragonflies and Damselflies did indeed seem to be on the up in the UK. Studies in recent years had shown around a 40% increase in their distribution, while only around 10% declined. Current research now shows that we have apparently gained eight new species since 1995 and two others have reappeared after a long gap in their records.

In 2022 the UK had a record number of Jay sightings, an increase of 73%.

> 'When we feel joyful we feel young. We have achieved much despite man's best efforts.
>
> My Mother has relaxed more. She has put her house in order and all is well. I'm pleased, as is she.
>
> Evolution is a relative thing. We all evolve. Some of us evolve naturally, following our true path and not becoming bogged down in the smallness of living. Some don't seem to evolve much during their physical existence on Earth and so their lessons after life may be chosen for them.
>
> It's all about achieving perfection. Some people seem hell bent on avoiding it, like it's a bad thing. Some know they seek perfection and are prepared to follow their path to achieve it.
>
> So, some may simply follow the path, or some may be led and even sometimes 'pushed'; although those who fall into the latter category tend to fall by the wayside and repeat mistakes, which is such a waste of energy and joy. They fall into oblivion, re-emerge and we encourage them to follow the path, but some Souls are stubborn.
>
> Even I may have SEEMED to be stubborn in life sometimes, in that I lived my life on my terms, but I was only being true to myself. "Follow the path of least resistance" – that is Bernard's advice and, "go with the flow and

ENJOY the ride".

If you repeatedly encounter obstacles there comes a time you must sit and observe them carefully and ask what their lessons are. The more stubborn a person is in this life the more lessons they will have in the next.

So, we DO have a say in whether we learn the lesson (because we have free will), however we have less say in how those lessons will present themselves; be they tasks, messages or different incarnations, in order to see a different perspective... One would not have the knowledge to choose, therefore it may be chosen for us.

If we knew what we needed, most of us would do it – though not all, especially if the journey looks difficult or unpleasant. There are lessons to be learned in all things. It's impossible to remain positive at all times, but the messages and lessons we learn do uplift us once we realise what they are.

I shall help in editing my book, you go ahead and write down everything you need to remember. I will edit out what isn't necessary – via Clare because she doesn't know us well.'

And I can state categorically, that's exactly what Bentley did while completing his book; he sat at my shoulder, nudging me to remove a sentence here, add a nuance there, and I simply did as I was instructed!

'My dear mother, OF COURSE this was meant to be – us being together and continuing our relationship in new ways after my departure. We were always destined to be together and well, some aspects of our life together were engineered or directed to arrive at this point. Trust me always. I will never misdirect or misinform you, ever.

Remember to celebrate and remember to hold on to joy. I love you Mother and have nothing to chastise you for.'

Janet: Bentley had said he might have SEEMED stubborn. Was Bentley stubborn? I don't think so, just pretty well perfect as far as I'm concerned. We suited each other well and I did not interfere with him living his life as a cat EXCEPT when it came to a visit to the vet. I am sure most people who live with an animal will understand this. An emergency visit to the vet is very traumatic but also a routine visit can still be most upsetting.

Stage one – I had to consult the five-day weather forecast. Was there any chance that the weather would force Bentley to stay indoors? If so, that was when I would make the appointment and keep my fingers crossed. This rarely worked so it was how soon I should start trying to get him indoors? Too soon and it caused additional stress, too late and there was a good chance he would not turn up in time.

Stage two – Providing I was successful with stage one of the exercise, stage two meant Bentley became aware of what was about to happen so he hid, and I'd try to find him. This frequently involved considerable moving of furniture, and the clock would be ticking down to appointment time.

Stage three – This was about getting Bentley into the carrier. Limbs everywhere and something akin to rugby tackles took place. On no account could I release my hold on him. On no account could I weaken and give in to him.

During each stage there was always the possibility of having to call the vet to cancel, but providing I was successful I then had to come to terms with my guilt at doing this to such a wonderful creature. Who was the most stressed by the time we reached the vet? Difficult to say. Who was always the amazed one after the visit? That would be me, because I would inevitably be forgiven.

Eventually, due to Bentley's thyroid issues the vet wanted to check him out on a monthly basis and we both became used to the routine. On one visit there was none of the usual blood tests or claw clipping or anything else required. 'Going home Bentley' and he took a nose dive into the carrier. As soon as we got indoors he did an about turn and headed out. Within 24 hours three of the neighbours spoke to me to say they understood that the trip to the vet had been successful. It turned out Bentley had found most of the neighbours and with his body language, obvious excitement and meowing he had managed to make them all understand that he had got one over on the vet.

One December the vet's office presented me with a diary. It was explained that every year the top one hundred clients – as in spend – were given a diary. However, it was extremely rare that a client with only one animal ever made the top one hundred! Personally, I think Bentley should have been given a medal.

Chapter 18

Hearts are Opening

Janet: Four weeks before this conversation took place Pippin had gone missing for 34 hours. Searching for a day and a half produced no results but he finally arrived home in the early hours of the morning. How he managed to get home I did not know and there followed the nightmare journey to the nearest emergency out of hours vet, some 15 miles away. I knew things did not look good, as confirmed by the vet who said it was probably a road traffic accident, and I was advised of the options and the problems each one involved. It was not a decision I could take time to make. I had to play God and for Pippin's sake asked that we let him go. There was a better life waiting for him. My last words to him were 'find Bentley, darling'.

Bentley began this session by immediately addressing the tragic passing of Pippin.

> 'Firstly, you need to know that Pippin is safe and well. You must know that I would never let him cross alone. I helped him get back home to you because I know you wouldn't have believed me if I just told you what happened without you seeing him with your own two eyes.
>
> I explained to him his options; pain, suffering, strangers and medicines that may not even work, or peace, tranquillity, joy and freedom, and he chose to come with me. I didn't tell him to, he made his own choice.

> Likewise, you are not his executioner.
>
> Many humans overplay the role they have in the life of animals, particularly when end of life issues arise. They claim they 'made the decision' when it is often the first time they have actually ever listened to the desires and needs of their pets. Remember, we animals do not fear death, only needless pain and suffering. Pippin was distressed because of pain and not from fear of death. And I was with him to make sure his transition was easy and gentle.
>
> You did well by him in his short lifetime and he is no longer your responsibility. He thanks you for rescuing him and for loving him so much. His life was good with you but he'd already lived a lifetime in his few short years. Don't overplay your part in the end of his life.
>
> Ego makes you feel it was your fault when in fact he takes full responsibility for all his decisions that led to his demise. YOU did not cause it. I did not cause it and even the driver did not cause it. Pippin made an error of judgement, nothing more, nothing less. No divine punishment for bad behaviour or thoughts. It was a mistake, an unfortunate outcome and then ultimately a decision to leave his suffering behind, that's all.
>
> Now, are we done speaking of him in MY time?'

Bentley always knows how to end a conversation thread and bring the attention back to the star of the show, the cat with the appointment to chat!

Janet had asked Bentley for more clarity about the writing of his book and yes, the subject of publishing!

> 'The book will be ready when it's ready and when OTHERS are ready to hear my messages. My words are sacred to you, I know. They're my gift to the world but some people aren't ready for my gift yet and could reject it. Times are a-changing, minds are developing, and hearts are opening. It will be their gift when the time is right. Don't devalue it and don't give it away. Think of the good we can do.'

Bentley was referring to the good that can come from his decision that proceeds from the book go to charity, in addition to the gift of his wisdom of course!

> 'Don't worry, I will make sure you don't forget anything important, and I will guide the hands and eyes and hearts of you two and those who work on it with you.
>
> Don't worry about it so much. You worry your life away instead of taking pleasure in every minute. Of course, you are allowed time to grieve but remember, you grieve for yourself. Pippin is fine and does not grieve. He's now having his own adventures.
>
> The rainforests are offering the most protection and the most healing for the planet right now. Rain, rain, rain, washing away impurities, bringing new life in every droplet.
>
> The Elephant Kingdom shall rise up. Matriarchal society will restore balance and peace. They will not tolerate or suffer abuse for much longer. It's time to restore balance. We must honour them – female Ganesha, female elephants, matriarchal, loving, guiding energy – not patriarchal violence. Not musth.
>
> Love and peace.
>
> No more shackles. Co-operation, not control, in all walks of life. This is the way forward.'

When Bentley speaks of a female Ganesha I believe he is referring to the Hindu goddess Vinayaki who is often depicted with an elephant head and woman's body; the female version of Ganesha. In Buddhist tradition she is known as 'The Heart of Ganesha'.

Musth refers to a rise in testosterone levels in the bull elephant's body characterised by a spurt in energy, which causes the animal to feel more restless and energetic, with heightened aggression and unpredictability. Musth is perfectly natural in a healthy bull elephant, but as Bentley points out, masculine aggression is not something the world needs right now – rather we are in need of matriarchal nurturing, love and compassion.

I also believe that when he states, 'No more shackles' he is referring to the fact that bull elephants used in tourism and other industries will be beaten with bullhooks and shackled with short, heavy chains in an effort to control them and to prevent them rampaging and possibly injuring their captors. And as Bentley says, co-operation, not control, is what these magnificent beasts need from us and we need from each other.

> 'And so, for now dear Mother, peace, rest, forgiveness and love. It's not your time to join us so make the most of your physical incarnation. We all love you. I love you and that's that.'

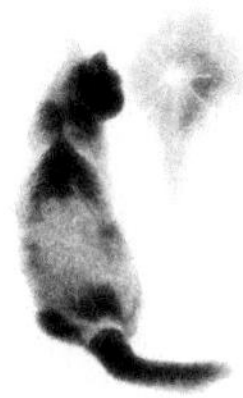

Chapter 19

Embrace Your Imperfections

Janet: I still had one nagging question – why was it me who instructed the vet to let Pippin go? Supposing Pippin had not made the choice he did, and I had still gone ahead with my instruction to the vet? I apologised to Bentley for once again taking up OUR precious time asking about Pippin.

When I connected in with Bentley, he was looking chipper and almost mischievous, with a happy kittenish air about him!

> 'I don't feel in the mood for great philosophies or theorising today. Today I feel like having fun – feline fun!'

I asked where this kittenish mood was coming from?

> 'We were all super busy last night with our wonderful Mother Moon, creating spells and making magic happen. So today feels like a 'day off' if you like.'

The previous night there had been a Super Moon, and I was intrigued to learn more about the magic and spells they'd all been creating.

> 'We were creating bigger and better shields for those creatures we have hidden, and we were helping those who recently transitioned to this level of existence because some do arrive confused and concerned.'

Bentley explained this was mainly farm animals and some wildlife and animals whose deaths were sudden and unexpected. Naturally, to leave this life suddenly and without warning would cause confusion for any Soul entering Heaven, even with their own guides to collect them. So having help from the collective of good Souls must be incredibly comforting.

'We reassure and welcome them into our family. It's like a Full Moon Initiation.

I want my Mum to have more fun, to give herself some 'time off' – from being so intense I think I mean. I love her and I love her attachment to me but whether she likes me saying this or not, I am NOT the be-all and end-all of her world. We are each on this Earth to continue or complete our own life story, not just to be part of someone else's.

Tell her to embrace her 'imperfections' and to not apologise or make excuses for herself. She should take time to be kittenish like me. She gets offended when I talk about her as she feels it's 'wasting precious Bentley time'. Well, she must remember that SHE is a huge part of MY life too.

My dear Mum, WHY are you still second guessing your decision over Pippin? Sometimes we have to make brave choices on behalf of those we love. His brittle body was clinging on to life and he was struggling to leave under his own steam because he was being helped and willed to stay alive – does that make sense? Your 'decision' (if indeed it was *yours*) released him from medical intervention to keep his life suspended artificially in any way shape or form, whether by drugs, drips, or surgeries. Pippin is fine. You say you trust and believe me, so please trust and believe me now. However, you must ask him yourself whenever you feel ready.

Our Full Moon Magic is strengthening and rejuvenating the Earth. Do not despair.

I want to play today. I don't want to get into deep conversations or think too much.

> The children love to see what happens at this time of year.'

This conversation took place at the beginning of December 2017. Bentley revealed a seasonal image of glossy green holly wreaths, their scarlet berries gleaming in candlelight, along with colourful paper chains made by the children, who were all dressed up in their best outfits. Peter was in blue knickerbockers with a ruffled shirt and Charlotte in a pretty claret coloured velvet dress with a pristine white embroidered apron over it and wearing a lace ribbon in her hair.

> 'But the children are saddened at the inequality for children in other parts of the world. They want them to know they are valued too.
>
> I am well and happy. I love you Mother. Take a day off and have fun with me. Take a stroll down memory lane with me, recalling memories and looking at my photos. It will provide some levity for my book. Stories of my fun and kittenish side to balance my infinite wisdom.'

Chapter 20

A Stroll Down Memory Lane

Janet: Bentley had suggested a stroll down memory lane and that sounded like a good plan to me.

Bentley slipped easily into my routine of leaving home early for work and returning late. It was a routine he had been used to all his life. After five months with me I was made redundant, four years before I was due to retire. Being by nature a lazy person I was excited at the prospect of giving up work, although I perhaps needed a part time job to see me through those next four years.

My last week at work came. My last Monday. I was so thrilled. Bentley picked up on my excitement and I think was convinced I was not going into work, until the normal morning routine got underway. Once he realised that I was still going to work, being that it was the end of January and cold, he did his usual thing of curling up on the bed, and I felt he seemed a tad disappointed. As the week progressed my excitement grew which Bentley decided to ignore. He was not going to allow himself to get caught out again!

The following Monday, the first day of the rest of my life, I had things to do and people to see so I left home at the usual time, leaving Bentley once more curled up on the bed.

However, I returned home three hours earlier than usual. He looked up at me and the sheer joy in his eyes was overwhelming. Perhaps it was then I realised that cats *could* get lonely too. Having been offered two part-time jobs I turned them both down. We would manage, and we did. What was money compared to the gift of those extra four years to be there for and with Bentley when he wanted or needed my company?

The start of February that year burst forth like late Spring, warm and sunny. We both spent most of our time outside, me gardening, Bentley supervising – plus I also got some work as a jobbing gardener for two of my neighbours. This meant Bentley could come as and when he felt like it. Could life get any better? No! Doing work I enjoyed, often with the company of my lovely boy, was bliss.

It was in February that I had to come to terms with taking Bentley to the vet for the first time. He had a cyst under his eye that needed to be removed. The vet said his fur might not grow back in that area, but it did. It came back white, not black, so ever after he had a silver streak under his right eye.

I also recalled the sudden appearance one early summer day of what seemed like hundreds of Red Admiral Butterflies, all 'wanting' to be chased, and of course Bentley obliged!

Bentley knew all the neighbour's names. I would tell him who I was visiting and if he really liked them, he would come too.

He also knew the word 'rubbish'. I would shout it out and he would be there. We would stroll to the bins together and on the way back he would race and hide. He always loved a game of hide-and-seek. He would jump out at me from the shrubbery, and I would be so surprised!

After my retirement our routine changed; there was no routine. Life became more relaxed and flexible, and we developed traditions instead. At some point early on Bentley, I think, decided to find out where the goal posts were. He wasn't challenging me, just checking how much he could get away with. He jumped on to the dining room table and stared me in the eye. It was like he was saying 'What are you going to do about this? How are you going to remove me from the table and with whose army?' On the other hand, he may have just been asking for some attention. I gave him a big sloppy kiss on the top of his head.

Next, he jumped on the coffee table with that same challenging look in his eyes. I sat down on the couch and put my feet on the table. He balanced his way along my legs and plonked himself on my chest. That was the start of our evening tradition. Bentley on the coffee table meant 'sit down Mum, turn on the television and relax, while I practise being a tightrope walker along your legs'. Sometimes he would wedge himself between me and the arm of the couch then wriggle me along inch by inch until he had enough room. Succeeding in shifting an eight stone something woman gradually along the couch is pretty impressive.

It was the same at bedtime. How can a small cat stretch like elastic so that I would be scrunched up in one corner of the bed? Or even worse, wake up to find myself hanging off the edge like someone about to jump from a tall building. Many a time I rolled off the bed to the floor, picked myself up, walked round and climbed back in from the other side!

Bentley was a cat of few words. I talked; he did body language. We understood each other. He found out very quickly that there were no goal posts. It was his home to use as he wished.

'A cat of few words'. Oh the irony. I did chuckle! (Editor)

From time to time, as anyone with a pet will understand, a trip to the vet was necessary. On one occasion though it was to have an operation to remove a thyroid gland. There was much soul searching before I made the decision. There was no sleep for either of us the night before he was due to have his operation: Bentley, because he was not allowed out (and to add insult to injury, was not allowed food either) and me, because Bentley was not a happy chappie. No food the following morning and to my horror he was so desperate he started eating the fresh cut flowers in the house. I made a mental note never to have real flowers ever again and deposited Bentley with the vet.

After several hours of pacing and worrying, a phone call came through at 2pm to tell me I could collect Bentley between 4 and 6pm. I would leave it until 6pm as I knew they would make me keep him indoors, and the fewer hours I had to do that the better. Somehow, I found myself standing in the vet's reception at 4pm clutching the carrier. The nurse told me he could not go out for ten days. WHAT?! Bentley would not last ten hours with such restriction!

Another sleepless night for us both. The following morning my neighbour offered me a small harness and lead so I could at least take Bentley for walks – splendid! I put the harness on very carefully and made sure none of the straps went near the wound. Lead attached, we headed out. Once the front door was open Bentley ran full speed dragging me along after him. Suddenly he did a sharp right turn and crashed into the shrubbery. I was yanked sideways; my feet left the ground. I sailed through the air and landed face down in a lilac bush! I was still clutching the lead which was now hanging limply, and the attached harness was, of course, empty! I removed myself from the bush and watched as Bentley raced and jumped around the garden like a spring lamb. So that was that, he was out. I watched him like a hawk, the neighbours were alerted and patrols set up, binoculars dusted off. As closely as possible every move was monitored.

Three days later we had the post-operative appointment.

'Just keep quiet' I said. 'We will admit to nothing! Are your paws clean?'

Never in the history of veterinary medicine can a vet have seen two such innocent faces looking at him. Finally, he said 'I know what Bentley is like and I think you can allow him out now'.

Before the vet could change his mind, Bentley was in that carrier and we were out the door quicker than landing in a lilac bush!

🐾 The time came eventually when Bentley needed pills twice a day. There are many jokes about how to give a cat a pill but they cease to be funny when faced with the situation, especially for the long term. Of course, when the vet pops a pill into a cat's mouth it is done in the blink of an eye like some impressive party trick. For most of us trying the same thing at home just does not work, because:

1. The cat is already on the table
2. You are hanging on to your cat like grim death while the deed is done by the vet.

To attempt the same thing on your own is unlikely to be successful. We just do not have enough hands!

For a few days I managed with hiding pills in cream cheese but that did not last long. Bentley is no fool. This was followed by fighting, confrontation and attempting to impose my will in order to ram a pill down Bentley's throat. He started to avoid me and why he even bothered to stay is quite beyond me because in his eyes I had been completely unreasonable about the whole situation.

After three weeks we were both frazzled and I was very aware that things could not go on this way any longer. A different approach was needed. Somehow or other it had to be turned into fun. I sat on the floor next to him and explained everything, then proceeded very slowly and gently to tip his head back, pull his lower jaw down and put the pill in his mouth as far back as I could get it. This was quickly followed by a couple, or four, treats.

We were once again a team, working together and that is how it continued. Bentley liked me to take time over it, to give him a cuddle and a few kind gentle words. The blink of an eye party trick was not for us. When it was time for his pill he would come and find me to remind me about it. Occasionally he would like to tease me by spitting the pill out as far as he could, and on one or two occasions I would find a pill stuck to a cushion in the living room, but, this was just his little joke to remind me of who was actually in charge around here.

There was the day I brought home some fish and chips. It was beautiful weather, so I sat outside on the patio to eat them. Bentley had never seen me eating outside before and I watched him, eyeing me with fascination, in between being handed treats of cod! Okay, most of the cod. I ended up with the batter and the chips. I could almost hear his brain taking everything in and working through it. That was a bit of a turning point. Ever after, unless the weather was very cold, *he* had to eat al fresco. It did not matter if it was the front or the back garden, but it *had* to be outside. The exception was the dried food left down for grazing purposes, especially if I was out. Well, when needs must…

Then there was the year we had ten inches of snow which did not impress Bentley one jot, although he hung around

long enough to watch me build a snowman. However, Bentley did love Christmas. It was the tree in the living room with its shiny baubles. The presents underneath it were a fascination. He did just about everything except pick them up in his paws and shake them. Cards were signed – from Bentley and Staff. By the time Christmas Day arrived he was pretty bored with the whole thing but would curl up nearby as I opened our gifts. 'Toys Bentley?' Oh yes, that was more like it. Normally he did not do toys, but Christmas was the exception. Usually he preferred the real thing, as in a mouse, or alternatively, honing his skills with evening 'practice mouse', which just happened to be my hand. That was the only time things got rough and it would last about ten minutes. Enough to mean I had almost permanently scratched hands.

Sometimes mice could be a problem. If one had been brought indoors and managed to find safety behind some furniture Bentley did not believe in wasting time on them. He just went back outside and found another one, leaving me with the problem. There are of course several ways to handle this situation, none of them very nice. The offending mouse, who after all had not asked to be dumped in our home, would indeed make himself comfortable, taking a liking to Bentley's dried food and mainly stockpiling it behind the cooker.

My home is no place for a wild mouse to be and they all, in turn, had to be removed. I came up with what turned out to be a very successful and simple solution. I would wait until dark, open the back door, turn all the lights off and sit in complete silence. If boredom set in, I'd read a book with the aid of a torch. Given a bit of time the mouse would emerge from their safe place and scamper out through the door into the darkness of the night.

Before I stumbled upon my master plan, mice would sometimes reside for several days and truly settle in for the long term. Some would make neat piles of dried cat food behind the cooker and some would chuck it there in a more haphazard way. One mouse I became quite fond of would come and sit by the computer while I attempted to send emails. What a time waster he was. I would sit fascinated as he washed his face no more than a couple of feet away.

Of course, I had to be careful who I told such stories to. Those not used to cats can be quite horrified. Those with cats as companions accept it all as part and parcel of daily life and indeed have similar stories to tell. I suppose if Bentley and I did not have a 50/50 relationship I could have made a mild complaint – but we did, so I didn't.

They say that cats bring home mice as gifts. Not sure I really believe that but maybe they are doing their bit to provide food? Sometimes though I really think Bentley did bring a mouse especially for me. Like the time he kept insisting a mouse stayed in my slipper. The mouse had other ideas. Or the time he placed a mouse down in front of me and stepped back. We talked about this mouse, and we agreed (I think) that maybe he could still live outside. I picked him up and Bentley came with me as I put him out the back door. For several days that mouse would run around the patio in broad daylight. Bentley, who so easily could have caught him would just sit there and watch. Mum's mouse!

Life is never dull with a cat!

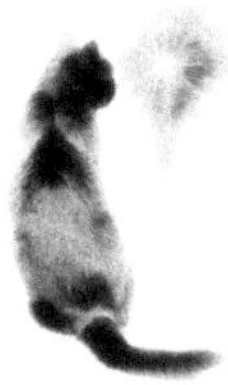

Chapter 21

Nose Prints from Heaven

On Bentley's instruction, Janet decided she would like me to speak with dear little Pippin for her, to make sure he really was okay on the other side.

> **Janet:** I hope you don't mind my speaking to you. It is just to say I only ever wanted you to be happy. I can't explain how distressed I am at how everything ended for you and for both of us. Thank you for the precious three and a half years we had together and thank you for getting home to me. Just because you are no longer with me does not mean I no longer love you or care about you. Pharaoh (the cat who lives down the road) misses you, as do I, but Bentley tells me you are okay and happy which is what is important. Please tell me how you are getting on and remember you are my precious, gentle, lovely Pippin.

Pippin was eager to speak and glad he had the opportunity to explain to his Mum about where he was now living and to tell her how he was faring after such a sudden end to his Earthly existence.

Pippin: '*The end of my life was such a jumble. I was so scared and hurt after that big thing hit me.*'

Pippin showed me a flash of silver approaching, a hard impact and then pain and confusion, confirming he had indeed been hit by a car.

Pippin: '*I didn't know what to do. I ran around panicking – I think that* *was adrenaline, but I was running in circles and not achieving anything but panic. And then Bentley came to me. He stood right in front of me and stopped me running in my tracks. I was scared at first. I thought I was going to get beaten up, but he hushed me, and he put a paw on my shoulder and stopped me and calmed me. He kept his paw there until my breathing and heart rate slowed down. My eyes were like saucers.*

Bentley told me I had two options:

One — I could go with him now, not look back and be free of pain and fear. (I liked that idea but was scared of what else there might be.)

Two — to go home and ask Mum for help. I was so panicked I didn't even know the way anymore. I had lost all sense of direction. But I wanted to be with Mum. She would know how to help me. She always knows what's best for me and she always does what's best for me.

Bentley said he knew the way home and he would guide me. He also taught me how to lift free of my body when the pain was too bad.'

Animals have this ability when they are chronically sick or in great pain, to lift their consciousness free of their physical bodies so they don't feel the worst of the pain. I've witnessed this countless times in animals I've worked with. The animal almost appears to be deep in meditation – or unconscious, but their soul is hovering just above their physical body, taking a rest from the pain before re-animating it again, or leaving it behind permanently if that's what's best for the individual.

Pippin: *'My insides were all in the wrong place. Some were pushed up under my diaphragm, my ribs were making a grinding noise, but Bentley guided me all the way home like a bright star. I'm eternally grateful to the point of annoying him! But truly he was the light in my clouds. He squirms when I call him an Angel but that's what he was to me.*

I'm so sorry I gave you such a shock but I'm so grateful you listened and let me go with no pain or fuss. I only came home for that and to say thank you and good-bye.

I know you miss me. I miss your voice and the way you did everything for me. I don't miss being mortal, or other humans though. The entire existence was too confusing for me. You were the best part of it, and you made my life matter.

You're a good friend AND Mother. I won't ever be a cat again. I can't say I liked much of it apart from playing with my friends and you, but even then, I was not always the best judge of character.

You have seen me out of the corner of your eye and saw me against your legs, but is it okay if I don't visit very often?'

Pippin was just getting the hang of being in Spirit form and was settling in nicely in Heaven, and, as part of his physical life had been miserable before meeting Janet, his preference was to stay where he was, comfortable and calm and free from fear.

Pippin: *'I send the square of light on the wall and black hairs and black whiskers. I asked Pharaoh to keep an eye on Mum and I'm leaving nose prints on the window.*

I know what love is because of you and I love you too. You are my sunshine as much as I was yours.'

Pippin drew a great big kiss which he asked me to pass on to his Mum for him. He also asked me to send (on an energetic or psychic level) two gifts; rose quartz crystal and forget-me-not flowers.

Rose quartz is a beautiful pink healing stone and is known as the stone of unconditional love. It attracts love to those who carry or wear it and encourages self-love. This crystal calms and heals the mind allowing you to let go of worry and fear. It helps heal old emotional wounds and prepares you for future love. Rose quartz envelops you in pure love, helping you regain trust in others following an emotional hurt, by dissolving the toxic emotions of anger and resentment.

In plant lore, Forget-Me-Nots represent true and undying love, a remembrance after death and a connection that lasts throughout time, reminders of your favourite memories or time together with another person. They also represent fidelity and loyalty in a relationship, despite separation or other challenges.

> **Janet:** Until this talk with Pippin (and the previous one with Bentley), it had been a mystery to me how he had ever managed to get back home. The nightmare of getting him to the out of hours vet, being told the damage to his body, and that if he survived long enough they would not be able to do an x-ray for two weeks. I could not put him through that with little chance he would ever be the same again. I said just three words, 'Let him go.' I turned back to Pippin, 'Find Bentley, darling'. I held him in my arms after the deed was done and then made the necessary arrangements. When I walked out of the vet's office it must have been about 3 or 4 am. I just stood there on the street unable to think straight and that was when I cried.

Janet and I struggled with whether to share this conversation with you, but when I checked in with Bentley prior to publication, he insisted it was needed…

> 'It makes sense of Pippin's story and is also reassuring about the dying process. No-one ever crosses alone, isn't that reassuring, and a comfort? There is always help and a guide, however we find ourselves leaving our body, and whatever decisions we make at the end. I knew Pippin needed me, and I knew our Mum would want me to be there to help him. The same is true for every soul that crosses over, regardless of their home situation, and regardless of who might be already waiting for them, or not as the case may be; one of us, their family, your loved ones, or the children who now wait for the orphaned animals will always be there to help ease the transition. We want this knowledge to bring you peace.'

Chapter 22

The Orange Ones

Janet's messages for Bentley this time were:

> **Janet:** It was good to hear how super chipper you were the last time we spoke and about the wonderful work you have done recently.
>
> I think we need to know a little more about the Alliance (for the book, if that is possible.) I know you are aware I spoke with Pippin. He said he is eternally grateful to you to the point of annoying you, but you were the light in his clouds. You squirm when he calls you an Angel, but that is what you are to him! I just thank you for everything you have done for him. I hope now he will be able to build up his confidence.

'So, you're asking me questions again, being inquisitive. Well, it's good to keep learning. It's good you're appreciating what goes on behind the scenes.

Pippin is not annoying me. I know he appreciates me leading him to the light and helping him to adjust. We don't live in each other's pockets. He has not become my shadow. He's growing in confidence in himself and finding his own path. He won't incarnate in feline form again, because much of his feline life was miserable and frightening before he met you, so it's his choice to never repeat that again.

> So, you want to know about the Alliance? I want Clare to know she has been neglecting her duties in bearing witness to us! You think no one would care about your writings but you are wrong. It's not the right time yet but you need to gather information you receive from us until the time *is* right.'

Bentley was right. I had been neglecting my duties. Partly because I sometimes had other things to do at Full Moon, such as dancing or drumming or, Heaven forbid – sleeping, and partly because I did feel the only one ever to read my notes would be me, so what was the point? But as Bentley was proving himself to be correct in other matters, it was something I resolved to rectify.

> 'Last Full Moon everyone was hard at work, weaving our magic and making plans. The orange ones (ginger cat members of the Feline Alliance) had the biggest magical input this month and the moon even cast an orange glow!
>
> Their specific magic is all about togetherness, companionship, co-operation, being exactly where needed at exactly the right time and being a support for those leaving and entering the physical world. They appear where they're needed.
>
> Mum will make a ginger friend who will visit but not stay. Tell her, "you must not feed him, because he's not yours to keep, he's only visiting to offer you love".'

Lennox: Clare's Ascended Master of a cat, the Zen Buddhist in a fur coat she introduces in Chapter 2, and fully 'paid up' member of the Feline Alliance.

Chapter 23

Relate to me as a Pussycat!

Janet didn't have any real questions for Bentley this time, so he had free rein over whatever he wished to talk to us about.

> 'There's an important Full Moon coming up. There will be huge energy shifts and a marked interest in compassion for animals and the Planet. We are working very hard on this. Humans may believe that they are influenced and guided by the planets but who do they think influences THEM? If they'd only listen to the animals FIRST, we wouldn't need to work so hard now! However, I'd be bored if I was in retirement because I'm like my Mum!
>
> I haven't seen much of Pippin lately as I'm so busy and he is still learning about his true self and his destiny, but I will pass on your love when I see him, though he knows you send it anyway.
>
> The children are happy in their favourite season. They send columbines to you.
>
> You are following your Soul's purpose. You just needed a gentle nudge from a soft black paw in the right direction once in a while. Now just follow your gut. Follow the synchronicities and signs.
>
> You thank me every time for my love. We WILL see each other again. I will come to guide you over here, so you know where you need to be – WITH US.
>
> I won't give you all the answers because some of them you need to work

out for yourself for your own journey and self-esteem.

In writing my book you must include stories of my cat life. My messages ARE important, but some perhaps mean more to us three than to the wider population. People need to relate to me as a pussycat with funny or cute stories so they can engage more fully with me and my messages. No one likes a pompous stuffed shirt. Everyone loves a naughty, cute cat and I am capable of being both!

I was and am your ray of sunshine and people need to know that side of me; my playfulness, my humour, my cuteness and yet my ability to infuriate certain neighbours!

There is a story about my claws you could tell…'

Personally, I always love it when Bentley has instructions for his Mum. He really does look out for her, but he understands her personality so well, he often comes across as if he's lecturing her. Janet groans whenever I quote a sentence to her that begins Mum, or more specifically MOTHER, (try saying it an octave lower than your usual tone and in a rather posh voice!) because she knows she is about to be in trouble for something, or else is about to have some serious work to do. Cats have such an unselfconscious way of putting their human slaves well and truly in their place, and cosmic cats seem to be the supreme experts in this art!

Janet: Cute. He was always cute. The day he moved in and curled up on the bed for the night then woke me by jumping up and down on my head at 3:30 in the morning because he wanted to go out and there was no cat flap. That was cute. The second night he did the same thing at 1:30 in the morning, that was less cute. By the third night he had his cat flap!

As for his claws, well what comes to mind is when he managed to shred them, presumably doing a fast right on the concrete to get out of the way of a rather large dog fox. The vet was convinced he had been involved in a car accident and insisted on doing a full examination. No other injuries were found, thank goodness!

But, that fox and the shredded claws, well that was a saga in its own right! I worried about Bentley because the fox was huge, more like the size of a wolf. I always figure that living with a cat means the hearing improves to the point of detecting the slightest noise and whether it means trouble! I heard a slight squeak at the front of the house and dashed round to open the door. To my horror there was Bentley sitting like a statue and, towering over him, the huge fox. I stepped out and grabbed Bentley from under the nose of the fox and threw him in via the front door – he insisted on poking his face round the door frame in spite of my telling him to get indoors… 'Ooooo Mum!' was the expression on his face.

I attempted to shoo the fox away, no deal, then clapping my hands, still no deal. The fox, perhaps feeling somewhat cheated by now, decided to take things up a notch and started to snarl at me. I bared my teeth and snarled back. He turned and left… *Phew*!

For six days I had to go out with Bentley and he would not let me out of his sight. Something had to be done. Simple, we must feed the fox. I saved any wet food leftovers from Bentley on a daily basis, grilled sausages and cooked roast potatoes and anything else I could find. Not a case of what shall I have to eat, more a case of finding a decent meal for Mr Fox, and he was definitely eating better than me!

Every evening at the same time I would take the food down the path away from the house and Bentley came too. Pretty sure the fox would be close by and watching for the food to be put down, he would see Bentley giving him the meal. This went on for a long time until one day the fox no longer came round. As Bentley said, they had ended up with a fragile understanding that worked. You want food, you leave me alone. It was a win-win situation all round.

Then there was the phase he went through of playing with the hinge on the bedroom door. I warned him about that but did he listen? No, and one day a claw got stuck in the hinge. His idea of freeing himself was to pull on the limb as hard as he could, which I suppose had some logic to it. My idea, having got down on my hands and knees behind him, because the door was open and I was frightened to give us more room by closing it, was to push his limb towards the hinge so that I could, hopefully, unhook his claw. He pulled, I pushed. I pushed, he pulled. Even worse, I could not actually see what I was doing. Several minutes after this 'tug of war' started we got his claw free without any damage and that ended his interest in door hinges.

Going out could be a problem. Many times I was diverted because Bentley would spring out from behind a shrub and do his level best to stop me from leaving the territory. This was hide and seek in earnest. He often won. Other times I would explain how long I'd be gone for. 'Just half an hour Bentley,' and sure enough when I got home he would be waiting in the same place looking up the road for me. That is cute on his part, guilt on mine.

Early on I realised that Bentley did not take to catnip so I bought a pot of catmint from the local garden centre. I placed the pot in the garden and he attacked it. He wasn't taking any notice of me and the camera. My gift was a success. Catmint remained part of the garden planting ever after.

The neighbours… well, normally there was no problem and the neighbours were very fond of Bentley. One day though I did get a phone call from one of them,

'*Your* cat has done his business against my daffodils'.

I apologised and said I would speak to him immediately upon his return. She thanked me and replaced her receiver.

Another neighbour, another phone call,

'*Your* cat is asleep on my couch'.

'On my way'.

I raced as fast as I could up the road. This, after all, was the neighbour who owned those much maligned Dog Daisies. Bentley was curled up into a little ball fast asleep on her couch. Much against his will I picked him up and carried him home.

Then there was the neighbour who really did not like cats and made it her life's work to make sure Bentley did not enter her garden. Bentley made sure he *did* enter her garden! It was an on-going conflict. Unfortunately, this neighbour became ill, and I agreed to go in and prepare her breakfast while she was confined to bed. Bentley came too. I went into her bedroom, followed by Bentley, to get instructions. She stared at him.

'You don't mind Bentley being here while I get your breakfast, do you?'

In plain English that meant, 'he stays, or you get no food'.

I looked down at Bentley. He looked so innocent! He stayed there in the bedroom the whole time I was preparing the food, and we then left together. Not only had he finally cracked the garden problem he had actually managed to get into the house!

Chapter 24

I Miss Your Singing!

Janet: It was July 2018. The weather was hot and in my area we'd had no rain for 83 days.

> 'You humans are not used to dealing with this heat and this weather. You need to be more like cats. Nap in the hottest part of the day and play in the coolest. Have more liquid in your food and seek shade, and offer shade and clean water to everyone else who visits.
>
> Tell Mum I'm sending her butterflies. They represent transition. Time actually passes quickly, more quickly than you realise and those 'awkward stages' will pass, emerging into perfection and beauty. Yes, in her life too. I know she'll shrug this off from false modesty as always.
>
> I want to hear her sing again as she goes about her everyday business and she's not doing that at the moment. It makes me sad and I worry about her when she is in deep thought. My Mum has too much time on her hands at the moment and she creates problems in her mind. She needs someone she can share her thoughts with. Someone with no agenda other than friendship. Like an animal friend.
>
> The children are enjoying the freedom, the sunshine and the warmth it brings.'

'You mentioned last time that you don't have actual seasons in Heaven?'

'It's always sunny in the children's Heaven except when they want to jump puddles. I keep out of the way then. We get to choose how Heaven is for us.'

Bentley was yet again confirming what other animals in Spirit had shared with me, that once we leave our Earthly bodies we can create our own Heaven. For example, a rabbit once showed me his Heaven, which was fields and fields of emerald-green grass spotted with wildflowers and herbs, his rabbit friends, and 'Not a dog in sight!' Because for him the company of dogs would not be Heavenly at all. As Heaven is a state of perfection, a prey animal would not be expected to share it with a predator, to live out eternity in fear.

Some animals I speak with have friends from many species (just like Bentley does) but others prefer to simply have the company of their own kind, or to be in the care of kindly humans who also love their human family.

Whilst I don't channel messages from human spirits, animals will often show me the image of a human who is with them in Spirit. That human may be related to the animal's human family or be a good friend or loved one. They're always animal lovers, probably lived with animals themselves, and they're always caring, nurturing people who naturally gravitate towards any of our animal loved ones who cross over and need someone to care for them until we arrive.

'There is not much work going on now.'

'Are you on your summer holidays?'

'Well, it's not because of summer, that's irrelevant here, but because there is a need to batten down the hatches planetarily speaking. The planets are aligning with Mother Earth about her 'cleaning project'. We are taking more and more decisions away from the hands of humans to show them that if they misuse their 'free will' we take back the power and control. Earth is cleansing herself using fire, flood and eruptions and from this there will spring new growth, new hope and more animals emerging from the shadows. But will the humans take notice? That is the question.

There is a shift towards giving Nature more credit for her powers. Even stupidity has a purpose. It brings together the good people and exposes the bad.

Don't worry… it's all going to plan.'

Chapter 25

A Cosmic Cat Finds a Mystic Mouse!

In a previous conversation which had taken place in 2017, Bentley had informed us:

> 'You will both see my book published. I will make it so. Someone needs to bask in my glory! When the time is right it will all fall into place and flow smoothly. I will make sure no obstacles are placed in your way.'

And believe me when I say, he was true to his word!

So, Janet and I began going through all our notes from every session we'd had with Bentley, which was a lot easier for Janet than for me, since I have all my notes from *every* client, in notepads going back two decades; dozens, and dozens, and dozens of notepads, and not all in chronological order (until now!).

When we did begin writing his book we had no idea what to include and not include, where the story would lead us or what the overall message was to be, we simply trusted Bentley, and I think we were both a little intimidated to do anything else to be honest!

The basis of each chapter would be Bentley's communication, his own words, since it was *his* book. Then the two of us would separately write our own observations and additional information based on each session. After a few more conversations Janet and I believed the book was more or less complete, apart from some additional notes from us both. It needed some tidying up and editing, but neither of us had any clue how to go about getting it published. So, the manuscript, such as it was, was put away on a shelf. Occasionally we'd mention it to each other, and wonder when it might be seen by anyone other than ourselves.

As I've already said, neither of us had any clue about the publishing process. I took quite a few courses on finding an agent or publisher, and on writing book proposals, which was where I always stalled. What kind of agent or publisher would take on such a work? There was nothing around to compare this book with. How would we convince a publisher to take on such an 'out there' book? How would we even classify it?

I could hear myself saying, 'Oh it's about a cat that died before I ever met him, and he talks to us from Heaven about how to save the world!' I couldn't imagine too many publishers knocking down our doors!

So, our notes and incomplete manuscript stayed on the shelf and we continued on with life, often commenting to each other that we still hadn't found the right publisher… and we continued to have frequent conversations with Bentley, following his new instructions, going back and forth between publishing options but developing inertia from sheer confusion and fear!

Then on March 21st 2024 (Spring Equinox) Bentley, during one of his regular conversations, berated us both for 'panicking and becoming confused, instead of trusting the process and focusing on finishing the writing of the book so that everything can fall into place as it approaches completion.' He continued to tell us the time was now for getting this project over the finish line, and that everything truly would fall into place if we just trusted him.

> 'Of course you feel overwhelmed. I've given you a huge responsibility, but listen to me, I would not have trusted you with it if I didn't feel you

could deliver exactly what I asked. And I wouldn't trust anyone else with my words, other than you and my Mum.

The important issue is to ensure no-one can change or misrepresent my words, or me. I don't say this in an egotistical sense but because I speak only the truth. Don't let anyone browbeat you, blinding you with their 'experience' or 'expertise'. Remember who the expert is here. If anyone makes you feel uncomfortable, they're to be rejected. We only get one go at this.

I brought the two of you together for a reason – to be each other's cheerleaders, covering different ground and different audiences. The right people will hear my words, I have no doubt.

Mother, prepare all my photographs so we can see if any will work in book format.

The task is not as massive as you imagine, I won't let it overwhelm either of you. This book has three voices, not just my own.

The first step, the first pathway is the most difficult, then the trail will open up before us with beautiful vistas. If ever you feel overwhelmed call on me. If you need inspiration, call me. Gather together all the books containing my messages, check them all for nuances and additional insights. I'm sorry if I appear pushy or bossy but the time is NOW. You need a deadline. Release it around a New Moon so I can be part of the hullabaloo. What fun!

See me now, sharper than ever before. Ever present, pushing you and guiding you along. See me. Trust me.

I love my Mum and her devotion to my tale.'

Bentley turned to fix his glowing amber gaze on me,

'I love your willingness to be part of the journey with us. We are family. Our Star Family. One day we will all meet here in the Council of Elders, continuing our quest to save Mother Earth and all her creatures. You're already in the Feline Alliance.'

You may recall I told you previously about me sitting at Full Moon taking dictation from the Elders!

> 'Start talking about it again and joining in the rituals we show you. There is to be an upcoming solar eclipse. Dedicate your time and energy to my book.'

That same March evening, I was deleting some Facebook friend requests from random strangers, and happened upon one from someone I felt an urge to check out. I looked at her profile and saw we had friends in common and decided to accept the request. We began messaging that night and struck up an immediate friendship; we felt like kindred spirits.

It turned out she was the founder of Mystic Mouse Publishing. I casually mentioned Bentley's conversation that afternoon (as you do) and she was immediately interested in his book!

Within a week we were polishing chapters, had a beautiful front cover depicting Bentley in Andromeda in all his glory, and had landed on the runway towards publication, all around the time of the epic Solar Eclipse just as Bentley had predicted!

'Bentley's Book' was going to be published at last and our new-found publisher friend is as entranced with Bentley's insights as we are, and not interfering with how he is represented at all, just as he requested. Turns out she also has a strong connection with Andromeda, so became the purrfect new starry member of Team Bentley!

Note: Around this time there was much cosmic activity; a Solar Eclipse on 8th April, Halley's Comet & a 'Dragon' Comet, The Eta Aquarid Meteor Shower and a powerful New Moon. It's as if the Feline Alliance somehow had one or more paws in this! Now it was *my* turn to offer up a skywards pirate wink!

The Cat's Whiskers!

At this point we thought the book was more or less complete. (To be honest we'd thought that a few times before!) However, Bentley was quite clear he wanted me to go through every conversation again, including those that took place *after* we'd started writing the book as he felt I'd missed some nuggets! So, these final few pages share excerpts of other conversations, various pieces of wisdom and, some additional predictions Bentley wished you to know about.

21/5/2020 – Shaken like a Snow Globe

This conversation took place in the middle of the first Covid lockdown, a time when the entire world had seemingly ground to a standstill and the majority of humans were gripped with fear and apprehension, so it was good to hear about goings-on in Heaven to take our minds off everything. Janet had asked for some clarification on some of Bentley's previous messages and apologised for not always fully understanding everything he shared with us.

> 'Mother, I never feel impatient when you don't understand some of my messages. I realise that for the Earthbound, the mind can't compute what the eyes don't see and the ears don't hear, so I try to educate you as best I can, but I know sometimes it doesn't hit the mark. That's okay. If I explained everything now there would be no surprises later, would there? Some things you just have to discover for yourself. I want you to remember that everything has a reason even if mortals can't work it out. Just trust that it does. Sometimes something quite disastrous has to befall so something else (corruption maybe) can be revealed. It's all part of the plan and our plans ALWAYS work out!
>
> The world is being shaken like a snow globe, but see also how the beauty and glowing lights have emerged as other negative particles settle to the bottom to be buried. Fear, panic, isolation and denying oxygen and clean air are the dangers. But here's the delight… see how quickly Nature responds when humans stop interfering with her! She, and we, are taking advantage of this break from what some call 'normality'.
>
> Mother Nature is recovering (from what we term plundering of the land) in ways you can't imagine. We are working hard, cultivating, cleansing, nourishing, protecting. Why should we bother? You would imagine that knowing what we know it would be so easy to just let the Earth and all her inhabitants implode in human greed, lust and stupidity, but what would they learn? Nothing. And they don't get to come here (Heaven) until they're ready to learn. Plus, we love Mother Earth, and we have no interest in destroying her. The ideal outcome is to educate the human

> race to appreciate and care for her, and it's happening.
>
> Yes, there are still bad acts that happen. But the good, the positive, the REAL actions are healing everything and the good outweighs the bad. So, we're forcing a change, a big change. Nothing will be the same again, even if it feels life has returned to 'normality', because the old 'normal' is being eradicated and the individuals who strive to control everyone and everything else are being revealed, and now their own inventions and technology are what will cause their crashing undoing. How ironically delicious!'

Here Bentley was excitedly rubbing his front paws together, like the villain in a low budget movie! If he had a moustache rather than whiskers, I swear he'd have twiddled it!

> 'Humans need more Vitamin D, from sunshine. Why do they deny their largest organ this health and life-giving vitamin? They also need to explore the healing qualities of plants, flowers, clean waters, mosses and tree orchids – they are super healers.'

I agree with everything Bentley says here but know nothing about the use of orchids within traditional medicine. On researching I discovered that the medicinal properties of orchids were first discovered by the Chinese in the 28th century BC and that orchids continue to be used for medicinal purposes today, most commonly in the form of medicinal tea. Dried dendrobium is believed to possess medicinal properties that can assist in strengthening the immune system and improving eyesight. It is also known for its antibacterial and anti-inflammatory properties.

Additionally, in Turkey, Saudi Arabia, Syria, and Iran, since the days of the Ottoman Empire, orchids have been used for making a traditional beverage called Salep made from the tubers of certain orchids. It is said to be effective in alleviating sore throats, digestive problems, diarrhoea and gum disease. I don't doubt anything Bentley tells us anymore, but I do find the research fascinating!

> ‘The witches of old will be pardoned but not only that they will be exonerated and celebrated. It will become a compliment to be compared with a witch.
>
> We are returning to ancient ways, indigenous ways. The circle is turning and returning to the healthful and healing traditions.’

Between 1692 and 1693 dozens of women were hanged for witchcraft and hundreds more were accused of being ‘witches’ at the trials in Salem. In May 2022 The last Salem ‘witch’ to be exonerated, Elizabeth Johnson Jr, was pardoned more than 329 years after she was convicted of witchcraft as part of the Salem Witch Trials. Great news for American witches, however the bill proposed in 2022 to pardon Scottish witches ended up being withdrawn in 2023 due to a technicality. Though, as we write, in 2024, a petition is still gaining ground to pardon the Pendle witches, and the Ministry of Justice has said ‘we acknowledge the historic injustices’. So the work continues…

Bentley is correct here, in that Janet and I weren’t keen to share predictions that at the time we had no idea would come true. Some of this stuff was out of our own remit and we had no clue how to present it so we wouldn’t look like cranks! (But how did we dare doubt Bentley and the Alliance?) As the months and years passed and I was able to look up some of these issues on-line, my excitement rose, and on sharing some of the predictions with long-time clients and friends I realised we had something incredibly special going on.

1/12/2020 – Jaguars and Brilliant Stars

I’m blessed to have had the honour of having had thousands of conversations with animals in Spirit and I loved being able to educate people about the visible signs to be aware of that their animals are sending; signs of their continuing love and devotion. Humans need physical, concrete signs, something they can see, hear or hold in their hands, since the majority have lost touch with their own telepathic abilities. If only everyone knew how easy it can be to continue conversations with their animal loved ones in Heaven.

Bentley has already described some of the ways he revealed himself and sent signs to Janet, but it feels appropriate to share some of the other signs animals have shared, that you may wish to look out for.

There can be the usual signs such as feathers and rainbows, which are both very popular because humans already know to look out for them, but there can be much more personal signs such as paw-prints, hairs (in the colour of the animal in Spirit), whiskers, flowers or leaves brought into the home. Also things like symbols in cloud formations, heart shapes in nature such as petals, leaves and rocks, messages in dreams and meditations and even retrieving lost items that have a link to the animal in question. There have even been animals who have taken over phone and computer screens, or sent their names on the sides of vehicles and number plates! Sometimes, it's in music too, though I do wish those animals wouldn't put songs into my head in the middle of the night, only for them to revolve like a vinyl disc on a turntable until morning!

I always explain to people that to send these physical signs uses a lot of psychic energy for the animal in Spirit; further evidence of the loving bond the animal still shares with their family to put such effort into reassuring them they're doing fine.

> 'I want to explain a little about how energy works from this side.
>
> Trying to manifest physical signs and visitations into YOUR plane takes effort. Lots of effort. It's why we don't just hang around visible to you all the time. (Well, also because we have completed our purpose in that lifetime on Earth so have new stuff to do.) Over here we have the energy to complete our tasks. There are times we use a lot, such as at Full Moon, or for special events, and we need to rest afterwards. But we don't work TOO hard, there is no reason to overdo anything. Energy does what it needs to when there's no physical body to move around. There is a natural balance.

We are still working hard behind the scenes to create a better world for those of you still living in it. There's a lot of unravelling taking place, lots you won't even be aware of.

Do not play Russian Roulette with your health. You still have work to do. You can't just cash in your chips and jump on a flight here just because you fancy it! You come when you are called and collected.

A special Jaguar emerges to raise awareness and help in conservation.'

Again, I returned to researching the information Bentley shared with us! In October 2020 a Jaguar began appearing on camera traps in Northern Sonora, Mexico for the first time and appeared to be making himself at home there. He was named Bonito (Spanish for The Beautiful). By 2021 it became clear that there were in fact two separate young male Jaguars, and hopes are raising that the Jaguars are moving North to reclaim old territory in the borderlands of Arizona and New Mexico where they once freely roamed.

As a result of these sightings, efforts are now being taken to protect Jaguar habitat, with calls to reduce or remove many of the barriers separating Mexico and Arizona to allow safe passage for the big cats.

In January 2024 a Jaguar was finally sighted in Arizona, becoming the eighth Jaguar in the US southwest in eight years.

Additionally in Brazil in 2022 a Jaguar cub was found alone, separated from his mother, and instead of going to a zoo or sanctuary, he was placed into a special scheme aimed at breeding and reintroducing Jaguars to the Amazon, and his reintroduction should take place in 2024. So Bentley could be referring to either or all of these special Jaguars, and the additional conservation efforts they have all inspired.

'There will be a new comet, very bright, and a sign of better times to come, like the original Christmas Star if you wish. But who will be the three wise men?'

Bentley gave me another of those devilish winks and his pirate smile. I'm quite convinced he doesn't believe there are that many wise men on Earth, so maybe we'll be led by three wise cats instead this time?

My research confirmed that in July 2020 comet Neowise thrilled sky-watchers in the UK as well as Europe and North America, as it was visible to the naked eye, and was hailed the brightest comet for 13 years.

16/11/2021 – Festival of Remembrance

As you can see by the date, Bentley dedicated this session to his observations of our annual rituals for those who died during wars and conflicts on Remembrance Day: poppies, wreaths, cenotaph services and the two minutes silence to remember those who died.

> 'Let me address your 'Festival of Remembrance', as I know Mum is intrigued. You may not find such a receptive audience for my words this time though...
>
> Yes, we animals observe humans taking just ONE minute out of their entire year to remember the 'Glorious Dead'. (By the way, there's nothing glorious about anyone leaving their bodies before their time and at the hands of others.)
>
> But also, ONE minute. You may say it's two minutes (silence) but let me tell you we see all the people fidget, minds wandering, unfocused. Most can't focus past ONE minute.
>
> Additionally, the world is in such a mess because of that ONE minute a year. "I've done my duty". "I've remembered them". "I bought a poppy" (of any colour) – but if they TRULY remembered they would work actively every other minute of the year to avoid another war or conflict. The people in all those wars and conflicts believed it could not happen on their territory in their time either.
>
> Complacency, laziness and stupidity. Humans are the WORST of all the

> species at learning from experience; instead handing over all their power to others to tell them how to think and learn.
>
> Please use your own brain. Learn from experience. Know that repeating mistakes over and over disappoints us greatly. So, yes, we observe your 'observance' with an emotion in the middle of sorrow and anger. It's an emotion humans seem incapable of registering, maybe because it would force them to change; because life could get a little uncomfortable if they face the truth of their actions and stupidity.
>
> But they don't realise that growth IS uncomfortable.
>
> Development hurts. Look at the caterpillar and the butterfly. The butterfly confined to that tiny space, crushed, uncomfortable, trying to grow in a restrictive compound. But see when they break free – the beauty, but not just that, more importantly the larger amount of space they occupy and the skills they never had before; they go from crawling to FLYING!
>
> Imagine YOUR potential if you just surrender to feeling uncomfortable and fight your way out to freedom. To flight. To realise your true potential to shine like the brightest star and bring joy to the world, before leaving easily for the next existence.
>
> Humans deny themselves all of this from fear, greed, apathy, and refusal to learn. How sad.'

22/2/2022 – Live in the Moment

> 'It doesn't feel like a long time since we last spoke, though I know for Mother she will feel it's been interminable! She lives in a different time zone to me.'

Here Bentley threw me a sideways huge grin, because he and I both know that quite clearly he's not just talking about distance or global proximity, but that time, as he's already explained, works differently when you return to pure energy.

'Thank you for letting me work over Full Moon and the solar flares. I needed all my concentration because you humans don't make our work easy sometimes. Humans really can be their own worst enemies.

Take today for instance, (22/2/22). I don't care what date it is but all these humans rabbiting on about what a 'Special Day' it is. EVERY day is special, why pin such great hopes on one day out of the thousands in a lifetime? What's wrong with the others? NOTHING.

Live in the moment – EVERY moment. Live each day as a surprise, a blessing, and an adventure. I feel like I've said it a million times. Maybe you need to tell more people!

However, that said, it's good to see humans finally standing up for WHAT'S right, not just THEIR rights. Speaking out to protect each other, not just selfishly defending their right to autonomy. Because sometimes co-operation, respect and peaceful discourse are needed.

Do you see those who choose to use force? So does everyone else now. Finally! Could THIS be the generation to finally change the course of humanity? We believe so. We have held important pow-wows about it around the Peace Fire.'

Bentley revealed a stunningly beautiful image of himself, plus many other species (some humans included), sitting in a circle, their faces illuminated by the flames of a central fire, their backdrop a moonlit indigo starry sky. Thoughts and ideas were being passed around the circle, flowing like a river round a rock. An image of an amicable circle of family, not blood related but united by a common cause – bringing back peace to Mother Earth.

'Trust your instinct in ALL aspects of life. Really, it's not complicated or mysterious. If in doubt, ask yourself,

"How does this fit with my belief system?"

"How does it make me feel?"

If it makes you feel uncomfortable, uneasy or angry at injustice for example, then you know, and ignoring that instinct would be wrong.

There certainly IS such a thing as divine timing, just not associated generally with 'magical days' like 22/2/22. That's human superstition and imagination all over again. Humans are SO suggestible!'

At this, Bentley threw his head back and laughed, before composing himself, lowering his gaze and gently shaking his head in disbelief.

'Look out for the asteroid; a bright, golden, cleansing flare – like Thor's hammer on those who would wish to control others! (Human and animal).'

It turns out that on the night of 22/2/22 the bright asteroid 1999VF22 did indeed fly by Earth and was tracked by many radars and telescopes. It was the closest approach it had made to Earth in over 100 years and is not expected to return for 128 years!

21/4/2022 – Free Will

As with every conversation, Janet had a list of questions for Bentley. This is natural because he tells us some mind-blowing information and leaves us to ponder it, and of course some of those pieces of information can play on the mind. She was (and still is) always interested in happenings in Heaven, and on what Bentley and all his friends were busying themselves with. Of course I'm fascinated too, but my role is to be Bentley's mouthpiece, and it's not my place to ask questions (though sometimes I can't resist if the subject matter is intriguing enough!).

> 'I would like you to spend less time on concerning yourself with happenings here rather than on Earth. We have everything here under control and we can be trusted to do our allocated tasks.
>
> On Earth there is still an element of free will and that necessitates us standing back and observing how humans will deal with certain situations. Ultimately, they must save themselves or not at all. And as you know, we will step in if necessary.
>
> We observe without judgement. Only humans bring human emotion into everything they do. We quietly observe and act accordingly only when necessary.
>
> Earthly existence is ultimately a learning experience. How can humans learn if we intervene every time they perform actions that negatively impact the world? We observe those who disagree with the negativity and work to right the wrongs. They simply work more quietly than the wrong-doers, which is why those humans observing begin to lose faith and become disheartened sometimes.
>
> Do not for one moment carry the notion that a war ANYWHERE means that evil has won. It's simply not true. You only hear what others want you to hear. Trust me, the truth is in the middle, not in either extreme.
>
> Also try to resist falling down the rabbit holes of convoluted 'do-good action campaigners' because they can often represent an ego power

struggle. Forgiveness is key here.

Ask forgiveness of those who wish you harm (they believe they are right even if they're not). Offer love and healing for their souls to access if they wish.

There is much positivity if you look beyond the smoke screens created by Man. So, focus on sending light and love through the smoke screens to help those who really need it.'

23/6/2022 – Befuddled

'I am feeling happy and sprightly today. We have had a wonderful time within the Solar System after a special Full Moon, a planetary alignment and the summer solstice. While not a celebration for us so much, the concentration of energy for good from around the world is incredibly powerful and reaches us too. It gives us faith in the goodness of humans in their intent and their love for Mother Earth.

Of course, the Earthly existence is a learning opportunity for ALL life, hence reincarnation and Karma. However, animals concern themselves less with the doings of others and walk their own path of exploration in the present. It's a much purer way of living and something that humans seem unable to achieve.

ALL cats are related, wild and 'domesticated'.

By the way, WE domesticated ourselves to help humans, they did not domesticate us! Humans neglected their telepathic powers and instead began relying on written language and symbols etc. What a waste of energy and ingenuity! We hoped, even if they could no longer speak our language and hear us, that they'd at least follow our example on how to live a Good Life.

You ask how part of an animal can still greet you even if they are once again 'alive' on Earth (reincarnated). You still don't fully understand energy flows and Souls. Just as part of their energy always remains with you in memories, reflections, shadows etc., part of them will know when

> you arrive (in Heaven) and need them. Just like when we sometimes send signs and messages when you need us in life, even though we're not physically there anymore. They just won't be around here (Heaven) as much because of their other duties; their attention may be elsewhere sometimes. It will all become clear when you arrive here. You're trying to run before you can walk and you are befuddling your brain.
>
> Out in Nature is where Humans heal, with the bird and insect sounds, the aromas, the sights and the peace.
>
> I love you Mother and I appreciate your dedication.'

13/2/2023 – Scientific Willy-Waving!

> 'I want to talk to you about the skies above you. The Heavens, the Universe, Space, whatever you want to call it. There is so much more going on than you could ever dream of; planets, stars, galaxies, universes. So much more than your human eyes and minds can perceive. We keep most of it a secret because we don't want mankind to 'discover' it and try to 'conquer' it. They've destroyed enough already. We won't let them manipulate and contaminate this pure and beautiful firmament. Their space exploration is pure egotistical folly. Scientific 'willy waving' if you like! It makes little impact on us or our presence here.'

Bentley constantly surprises us, but this time he also completely cracked us up! We even debated over including that sentence, but feel that by now you're ready for anything Bentley may tell you.

> 'The comet and the upcoming shooting stars signal a new era and an improvement or settling down in energy all across the world, despite what you may hear. Don't swallow their manufactured fear. Trust US. Don't worry about things outside your own personal world.
>
> I see you worry and get annoyed in equal measure. Trust me, I am by your side. This is your loving caring boy speaking, not the self-important Saviour of the Universe.'

Bentley threw back his head and laughed at the thought of himself as some cosmic superhero, before returning to his earnest expression.

> 'I can be both and I AM both. I'll always be your special boy and always with you when you need me. Just ask me and I'll accompany you. You don't have to be brave and do everything alone. Plus, then I can check what nonsense you are being told. Trust your instinct and trust me nudging you.'

17/4/2023 – Of Unicorns and Dragons

> 'The dark moon approaches. It is a time of rest, re-evaluation, release, and rejuvenation for all of us. The intensity of our work and developments eases off for time for self-care.
>
> You should follow our example. Not constant work, work, work. Peaks and troughs, intensity and relaxation. You cannot expect consistency of performance if your effort must be sustained consistently. You do not have the energy for that, especially Earth-bound creatures. Anyway, enough of that. Dark skies mean I can observe other celestial bodies as well as the moon.
>
> It is sheer folly to attempt to discover 'intelligent life' outside Earth! The arrogance of humans, they have no clue what intelligence really is. If they only knew how every animal and plant and rock and body of water carries more intelligence and wisdom than them! When they do realise, it will be too late for them, in that they will not know how to try to harness it. One day the true balance will return, and we will rejoice.
>
> I want you to know that creatures of legend truly existed, not just in imaginations – how could different imaginations in different countries all come up with the same creatures? I speak of the unicorn and the dragon for example. Humans are so arrogant to believe that it could be any other way.

Mother, you do know I understand your thoughts and motives even before you do, don't you? I do understand why you foster unfortunates but don't close off your heart to love just because you know they'll be moving on. You can still love them, and they love you in return. Love is love.'

To clarify, Bentley is talking about Janet fostering cats for a local charity.

'Mother, as long as you heed my important warnings and messages you will never disappoint me. Just do the best you can in all situations. You're intelligent enough to know what is best.'

12/6/2023 – The Maligned Souls

'I'm glad to see you enjoying the weather and the outdoors. It's so important for the heart and the Soul to get outdoors into nature as often as possible. Take a book or just walk or sit in the miracles unfolding around you, flowers unfurling, trees growing and animals living out their lives.

Thank you for protecting the more maligned; the fox, the rat, the squirrel. Now the mole needs our help. Poor persecuted souls.

The Earth needs a rich, diverse ecosystem and the humans constantly upset the balance, for either the native animals or plants, but then they malign the 'exotics' THEY introduced in the first place. What a waste of energy and all for ego's sake.

I'm needed here and you may well assist me when you arrive. And why not Mother? I love you and you've always said that you were my slave and that you'd do anything for me.'

Here Bentley roared with laughter, imagining Janet's reaction to this statement!

2/11/2023 – Balance and Growth

> 'Killing anyone for any reason is wrong. Letting people die due to apathy and greed is wrong. The planet provides enough for all her inhabitants if people don't hoard and become possessive. If people don't learn their lessons in this life they will in the next. Don't worry. There is a balance in all things. If you strive for balance in this life (for example if you have a lot, then donate or share) then you won't need to go through the lessons again. Fair is fair no matter how it is perceived in the moment. If you have no belongings or money or food to share you can share knowledge, stories, friendship and love. It's not difficult as long as it's genuine.
>
> You know, in Heaven you can be as busy as you want to be. I find my work intriguing and satisfying so I choose to work, and I have a good balance, like Bernard does. We know how to balance work and growth. The children could have the opportunity to grow up but they're so happy playing in the meadows, carefree and happy, that I can't see that happening for a long time, and why should they?'

Throughout our conversations, Janet often wished to ask after the children, to see how they were progressing and perhaps what the future might hold for them. Bentley was always happy to share snippets of their activities and their greetings, and an interesting pattern began to unfold as time progressed… the children and their link to animals in Spirit, in particular young or orphaned baby animals.

Bentley even shared with us a sweet day when he had no other business to attend to, and so, in his own words:

> 'The children are happy, as Pippin and I both took some time out to be 'petted' by them for a while, which we all enjoyed. They currently have a brown rabbit they care for gently and carefully.
>
> It was nice to have some time off work after the last Full Moon, and before the build-up to the next. I feel refreshed and reconnected with my inner pussycat when I'm with the children. Shhhh!'

Bentley held his paw to his mouth, his eyes twinkling, begging me to not give away his secret, that he's a real pussycat inside! I'd like to say 'your secret's safe with me, Bentley', but well, the cat is now well and truly out of the bag!

In subsequent conversations Bentley told me how impressed he was with the manner in which the children cared for the rabbit, then another puppy, as he explained:

> 'The (first) puppy has reincarnated as he hadn't had a real opportunity for a life. He's going to be fine and I'm sure will live to a ripe old age before he returns. The children understand and they can check in on him. They are so good with young animal souls, and I believe this will be their calling… they are so gentle and loving with them. The children most certainly do take care of the small and orphaned creatures and they bring each other joy and comfort. I feel they have found their purpose so have no need to return to Earth, nor to 'grow up'. They're perfect as they are, and blissful in their lives here.
>
> As time goes on, they've also cared for more orphaned bunnies, and a nest full of baby blue tits which brought great joy to all who observed; they fed them ever so gently and diligently. There are plenty of birds here to integrate them joyfully. The little blue tits happily fly around the children's heads as they look after more casualties. A baby rabbit, a robin chick, and some butterfly chrysalises. They do such a good job, and they are trusted with many new arrivals now. They love it, and each case has a happy ending.
>
> I am so proud of "OUR CHILDREN. OUR FAMILY". My heart bursts with joy.'

For Janet and I, who have followed the stories of these two special child Spirits for years, knowing they've found their Heavenly purpose, and can stay young, carefree, playful and yet also caring and loving, fills us with happiness and hope for all the other young and orphaned creatures (human and animal) who leave their physical bodies at an early age.

Over the 12 or so years I've been communicating with Bentley he would often use our chats as a 'Teaching Opportunity'. He would educate us on how things work in Heaven, share his own wisdom & philosophies and he'd even throw in some predictions for us; these were always exciting, but also always involved extra work on my part to subsequently research to find the evidence of each prediction. Not that I minded, as not everyone is lucky enough to be party to such amazing information and to learn the secrets of the Universe!

Bentley and I continue to communicate regularly, so there might even be another book, but for now we agreed to conclude with a selection of his highlights.

At the end of this session, Bentley showed me a fascinating image of the two of us, me with notepad and pen poised, hanging on his every word, and Bentley huge in comparison, towering above me, his amber eyes glowing against his inky-black fur. He was wearing what at first glance appeared to be a metallic gold elaborate collar, with three

panels coming down his chest and shoulders. As I looked more closely, I could see that the collar was not made from metal at all. He moved his head, and the collar left a golden trail. He moved again and it became clear that the collar was in fact made up of stars and starlight, so that when he moved his head or body, the starlight trailed behind.

No longer the small, cute kitty-cat, this was Bentley in his true magnificence, and I looked on in awe.

Predictions

26th April 2018

> 'The Nile River snakes are under threat by humans wanting to encroach on their habitat. They are grey smooth snakes with not much pattern to them and they blend into the mud and clay. Why can't humans simply co-exist?
>
> There will be a pink baby Hippo born in the wild.'

This conversation took place back in April 2018, and in November that year a man who had been photographing Hippos for 18 years spotted an extremely rare pink Hippo in South Luangwa National Park! The skin is pink due to a condition called leucism (the skin lacks pigment) and by all reports this individual was healthy and an accepted member of the Hippo pod.

I did some more research recently and discovered that in and by the Nile, Dice Snakes are non-venomous and live almost exclusively in the water, feeding on fish, frogs and invertebrates. Large groups of them mate in the river from March to May. The African Beauty Snake is another common water inhabitant, moving through grassy or reedy areas along the banks of the river, hunting for frogs, lizards, mice and smaller snakes. Dice Snakes are not considered endangered at present, though the Beauty Snake *is* classified as Vulnerable, however, they both suffer from loss of the wetland habitat in some areas of their range and also from pollution, roadkill, persecution by people, and collection for the pet trade. Thousands of snakes are killed every year in the nets set by poachers, and the recent increase in illegal fishing does nothing to help the situation.

Regardless of how you feel about snakes, Bentley's question, 'Why can't humans co-exist?' is extremely valid.

12th June 2021

> 'There will be a disaster in Space (well, one that the public hear about, there have been plenty more…). It will force them to begin work to clear Space Junk and those whose eyes had been previously focussed on making money through 'health' will shift to the lucrative recovery of Space Junk – this is a good thing for the Universe.'

I knew nothing about this, and as I was preparing sections for this book I began the painstaking task of researching, because, as previously mentioned, Bentley's predictions fascinate me and also, as an inhabitant of Earth, forewarned is forearmed!

What I discovered was that on 15th November 2021, during a Russian anti-satellite missile test, the Kosmos 1408 spacecraft was shattered into thousands of pieces causing fragments of debris. The crew of the International Space Station were forced to take shelter onboard to avoid being struck by pieces orbiting Earth which could have depressurised the station. Later, in June 2022, the space station was forced to execute a manoeuvre to dodge another debris fragment from the destroyed satellite.

Additionally my online research uncovered the following:

- NASA is tracking more than 26,000 pieces of space junk, which are endangering astronauts and space missions.

- Space junk can travel at 40,000km an hour and can destroy satellite communications.

- In Nov 2021 the Paris Peace Forum's Net Zero Space Declaration came about and by 2022 two UK based companies had begun designing missions to clear space junk.

- In June 2022 the UK government launched a Plan for Space Sustainability including a multi-million pound Fund for

Active Debris Removal. It's estimated that the global market for space junk will be worth $4.4 billion by 2030, according to a sustainability report commissioned for the UK Space Agency.

21st April 2022

> 'There is a new species of Hummingbird we will reveal, and their numbers are multiplying. The trade in exotic birds has been given a huge crackdown and a shift in how it is handled. So, there is much to be optimistic about and be grateful for.
>
> Even a 'new' dragon has been discovered where we'd hidden it. Of course, it's not new at all, it is quite ancient as all dragons are. We've simply hidden them for years.'

In March 2023 researchers in Cordillera Azul National Park in the Peruvian Andes discovered what they believed at first was a 'new' species, a Hummingbird with glittering gold feathers, but it turns out it's actually a never before documented hybrid of two different species - the Pink Throated Hummingbird and the Brilliant Hummingbird, who also has a pink throat. The researchers are fascinated to know how their offspring have a gold throat, as it is incredibly rare!

The 'dragon' Bentley refers to is undoubtedly some species of lizard, and my research uncovered a number of 'new' lizards had been discovered all over the world. To name just a few:

- The Liolaemus Warjantay found in the Peruvian Andes in September 2021
- The Khammouane Karst Dragon discovered in August 2022 in Vietnam
- A grey, yellow and gold lizard in the Andes in January 2023

- A new species of flying lizard named The Parachute Lizard in India in June 2023

3rd June 2022

> 'Kangaroo Rats are reaching new levels.'

In Autumn 2022 California was able to remove the Stephens' Kangaroo Rat from the Endangered Species list, mainly due to the efforts of a man named Joseph Messin at the Motte Rimrock Reserve who tracked and studied the Kangaroo Rats and their habitat in order to take measures to protect both, which seems to be succeeding.

> 'Jupiter, Saturn and the planets are all aligned (making an arch across the sky).'

A quick internet search confirmed that not only Jupiter and Saturn, but Mercury, Venus, Mars, Uranus and even Neptune plus a crescent moon joined in this celestial display on June 23rd and 24th, something that happens only once every 20 years or so, and on-line images do indeed show the planets in a wide arc shape!

12th June 2023

> 'There will be some spectacular sights in the skies. Even sights never before seen or documented in Britain in particular. We want humans to know this Earth is a magical place and worth fighting for – so not just meteor showers but colours and light in the clouds.'

In late June 2023, the UK saw not only sightings of some amazing Noctilucent Clouds in the skies, but up here in the North-East of England I saw and photographed iridescent Nacreous Clouds for the first time in my life! They resembled the finest Mother of Pearl and were stunningly beautiful.

9th August 2023

> 'Look out for a really bright coloured star or comet with a tail, illuminated against a black sky. It signifies happier times ahead.'

I discovered that at the end of August 2023 Comet C/2023 P1 (Nishimura) suddenly appeared in the night sky and was closest to Earth on Sept 17th, becoming easy to see even with binoculars rather than a telescope. Most images show it as green with a long tail, so I believe this comet may well be the one Bentley spoke of in earlier conversations too.

Also, in October 2024 many astrophotographers had captured exactly what Bentley described; Comet A3 ATLAS, which it's suggested won't be seen again for another 80,000 years!

And finally…

> 'I love my Mum and her devotion to my tale. I love your willingness to be part of the journey with us. WE are family. STAR FAMILY. One day we will all meet here in council (the Council of Elders) continuing our quest to save Earth and all her creatures. Clare, you are already a member of the Feline Alliance. Mum will have a job here too. Start talking about it again and joining in Full Moon rituals with us. There will be a comet or meteor shower when the book is released. It's all written in the stars!
>
> Now, I think we have enough material for the book.
>
> I love you Mum and I love you Clare.
>
> WHAT A TEAM! WHAT A TEAM!
>
> HOORAH!'

'I find it amusing that one day I will be introduced to a lot of strangers as a rather cute cat, only for them to discover I'm so much more than that, and so is every cat they've ever met!'

‘My dear family, remember there is something to be gained from every day, no matter how mundane the day may feel. By being fully present we see all the blessings, even the tiny ones, like a ladybird or a butterfly or a beautiful shaft of sunlight illuminating a treasure. Don’t waste a day reflecting on its emptiness but count the blessings, small though they may be.

Remember how I loved every day of my life. I was never bored, always finding something to interest me and make me happy. Live life like a cat. Rest when your body asks, eat only what’s delicious and life fulfilling. Find pleasure in the small everyday things that others miss. Find a reason to smile everyday even if it seems impossible, in fact, especially then.

My love,

Bentley’

About your Scribes

Janet Barber — Bentley's Mum

Janet very modestly states, 'I am certainly no author and I think of myself as a scribe for my beloved Bentley and HIS book'.

Janet spent most of her working life in communications and Human Resources. Once retired she started to teach Genealogy on a voluntary basis. After the loss of Pippin, Janet started to foster cats who were desperately waiting to find their 'furever' home. Sometimes she would have a cat for as long as three months, but there was always the inevitable heart-breaking day when the cat had to leave.

Janet says, 'I would constantly remind myself it was not about me; it was what was right for the cat. I would wave the cat off, close my front door and shed a few tears. Then it was on to the next cat who needed some help on a temporary basis'.

Janet was born and bred in London but now resides in leafy Surrey. She still offers talks, enjoys knitting for a couple of charities and, of course, adores cats!

Clare Metcalf — Animal Communicator

Clare is an award-winning professional Animal Communicator, Healer and Homeopath, based on the outskirts of Durham, England, with clients and students world-wide. She loves to write and to educate and had her own 2-page column in a hugely popular national magazine for 8 years.

Beginning her career as a Civil Servant, her working life was abruptly halted by a chronic illness that left her wheelchair bound. It was only through her beloved Homeopathy that she regained her health and discovered a new vocation as a Homeopath, ultimately leading her to rediscover her lifelong gift for communicating with animals.

Clare is an enthusiastic dabbler in anything arty, crafty, or creative, and she loves salsa dancing, live music, and theatre.

Together with her patient and understanding husband of 32 years, Russell, their wanderlust takes them travelling and hiking the great outdoors and exploring ancient and sacred sites. They live with their two rescued feline boys Jasper and Barney, with regular 'visits' from their now Spirit cats and rescue hen friends!

She is passionate about conservation, animal rescue and welfare and donates her time and expertise to many animal sanctuaries at home and abroad.

website: www.freespiritanimalcare.co.uk

Facebook: Clare Metcalf Animal Communicator, Healer & Homeopath

Instagram: claremetcalfanimalcommunicator

work for good.

During a conversation with Bentley on 30th May 2024 I asked him which charity he wished to support, and he stated,

"We'll not raise millions in sales, we all know that, but we will raise awareness where it's needed; that's all that matters to me. We need a charity that cares about conservation, not just of animals but of the planet, and everywhere, not just in one area. A charity that speaks out for the unheard voices; the voices of the animals, their habitats and the world in general. A charity that walks the talk, with integrity but also longevity. I have decided that we will donate to Born Free. They are passionate about cats of all sizes, and also many of my other friends. They care about the environment and Mother Earth. I trust them with MY legacy."

This news delighted me. I've supported Born Free since their inception, in 1984. Janet is also a supporter, and we both already sponsor animals with them.

Born Free's Compassionate Conservation aims to enhance the survival of threatened species in the wild and to protect natural habitats while respecting the needs and safeguarding the welfare of individual animals. They say, "We seek to have a positive impact on animals in the wild and protect their ecosystems in perpetuity, for their own intrinsic value and for the critical roles they play within the natural world."

- Born Free have created and work with sanctuaries and rescue centres to care for wild animals (often rescued from unsuitable environments and zoos) ensuring they live out their days in the peace, comfort, and respect they so need and deserve.

- They work tirelessly to bring attention to the suffering of captive animals in zoos, aquaria and in private ownership, bringing about legislation for better protection of wild animals and with the aim of phasing out outdated zoos.

- They campaign against the illegal wildlife trade, trophy hunting, canned hunts and so much more; working to protect many of the species Bentley cares so much about!

- They aim to educate children and young people about climate change, environmental issues and biodiversity loss, instilling a lifelong love for wildlife with the aim of protecting wild animals for the future.

So, you can see why Bentley chose Born Free – they're already unknowingly doing the work he tells us is required to save our Mother Earth!

Therefore, we are delighted to announce that proceeds of the book, Conversations with Bentley, the Cosmic, Conservationist Cat will be donated to Born Free Foundation via Work for Good.

A fitting legacy from a Cosmic, Conservationist Cat!

Free Spirit Academy™

Learning with Love

Clare's educational resource for animal lovers

Listen With Love™

Learn to communicate with your own animal friends!
For beginners and those seeking a refresher. Simple, clear grounding in focus, connection, communication techniques, active listening, etc.

Listen With Love Level 2™

For anyone who has completed Level 1 or has done some training elsewhere. Become more confident, proficient and spiritually aware, and deepen your connection with ALL species and all of Nature.

Homeopathic First Aid for Pets and People™

Covers all the basics needed to use homeopathic remedies safely and effectively for every member of the family, 2 or 4 legged.

Clare also offers various courses and seasonal masterclasses throughout the year.
See her website, newsletters and socials for details.

* 9 7 8 1 9 1 0 8 1 5 3 0 4 *

BV - #0094 - 191124 - C35 - 234/156/12 - PB - 9781910815304 - Gloss Lamination